T0146609

ENDORSEMENTS

To All Concerned-

I, for one, do not openly endorse things as a norm. This book is an exception to those thoughts. This book is an amazing journey through hell into happiness and peace in life for the author Lolo.

Abuse, violence, cancer, trials, tribulations and tragedy know no color or creed or gender. They attack any and all persons in and from every walk of life. What you do to change the tide of potential damage is up to you and in this book you will gain the inspiration, courage and dedication to God and self to combat obstacles that come against you. You CAN change your life for the better purpose. This book will be your role model to that change.

Read this book. Smile, laugh and cry during her journey. I did and I know her and a lot of what she has been through. Let this book mentor you to a stronger you with God and yourself. It takes a lot of work, but the end as you will see is well worth it.

Be a survivor. Be a breakthrough in your own life. Be your own healing process through devotion with God. Be your own journal writer and use those notes to better your own place and person.

May His blessings abound on all who read this book and take the lessons given to show you that you can change your life. Not just for the glory of God, but for your glory as well.

God bless you,
Lolo's Life Coach

The Journey Back to

LOLO

THE JOURNEY BACK TO ME

iUniverse books may be ordered through booksellers or by contacting:

iUniverse
1663 Liberty Drive
Bloomington, IN 47403
www.iuniverse.com
1-800-Authors (1-800-288-4677)

ISBN: 978-1-5320-3796-2 (sc)
ISBN: 978-1-5320-3795-5 (e)

Library of Congress Control Number: 2017918047

Print information available on the last page.

iUniverse rev. date: 12/20/2017

DEDICATION

This complete effort is dedicated to my late mother

1949-1993
I now understand that you did the best that
you could with what you had.
And…

To my grandson
2015-present
Honoring both my past and my future is what this work is all about.
I can in no way have one without the other.

CONTENTS

Epigraph

I MADE IT!

Understanding your journey means understanding your
value because from adversity comes advancement.

- Lolo

Book Foreword

I decided to write my own foreword for this book because of all of the books that I have written, this book is the nearest and dearest to my heart. From this work came a lot of healing, mending, deliverance and being set free. I never thought in a million years that I would, could, or should write a book about my life, but now I would recommend it for everyone. Sometimes this is all that you need to look back and thank God for where you have been.

Not everyone is fortunate enough to speak about the places that they have been and the things that they have been through from a place of healing. I wrote this book for my children and most of all for my grandchild/grandchildren. If I am never able to tell them what I have been through and peruse through pictures with them and tell them from whence they came, they will always have this book.

Another reason that I wrote this book is to help the millions of people out there who struggle with some of my same issues that I have overcome. I would that this book can serve as a testimony that if I made it you can make it too. God is no respecter of person and what he done for me, he will do for you as well.

The final reason that I wrote this book is for me. This book has enabled me to bring closure to a lot of events and occurrences in my life to allow me to experience a rebirth from a place of healing and deliverance from the bondages of my past. It also helped me to see the evolution of relationships that I have had in my life from the one with my immediate family to others such as friends, foes and even past lovers.

Through this work God has done an amazing thing and I hope that you enjoy reading it as much as I did writing it.

God Bless and Enjoy,

- Lolo

PREFACE

All of my life I have wandered through life wondering, "Why am I so different?" My thoughts, my actions, my beliefs, my rationale for life are vastly different than the next person. I am an avid researcher, I am committed to lifelong learning, I love ministering, I love singing, I love people to a certain extent, but at the same time I am a loner. I have presented myself to the world in the fullness of myself, as I knew it, only to encounter people who accept this part of me and neglect the other parts. For example, people would fall in love with the comedienne and expect me to always be in funny mode, but they don't understand the intricacies of a comedienne is the "not so funny" pains that they feel in the core of their being that are masked with their comedic elements. On the other hand, people would be attracted to the preacher in me and then when I make a mistake or want to go have a drink, then they think that I am phony or unsaved. I don't even want to mention the intellectual side of me that everyone loves, but then when it comes to matters such as street lingo and other concepts that just don't make sense to me, then I am judged as naïve and unintelligent or even worse, weak.

With these revelations, I came to the conclusion that if people were to accept all of me then they must know all of me. In order for them to know all of me, then I must discover all of me and share it, withholding nothing. With that in mind, God birthed this book, "The Journey Back to Me" as a tool for people who desire to know me and be used as an additional tool for them to get to know themselves. We become so that others may become as well. Our life journeys are not selfish because every storm that we go through is not for us, but that we may be able to relate and understand others in a manner of identification, as well as sharing the manners in which we overcome in an effort to help them to become better as well, even if it means us growing together. These are that truths that are not taught in school or church but must be understood in order for you to live your best, most authentic life.

Writing this book, reading this book and implementing the practices of its sister book, "Embracing the Journey: 40 days of Filling in the Blanks of Your Life" will save some thousands of dollars in medical bills and therapy costs because, if the truth be told, a lot of our health issues are related to the irritation, aggravation and debilitative ignorance of who we are. This does us a disservice and often forces us to fall prey to the satanic attacks of the memories of our past that cause us to feel victimized by this thing that we call "life". Then we encounter preachers who tell us we are the head and not the tail, above and not beneath but we are buried in the sands of our being and don't know which is heads or tails. So ultimately we fall into the antics of shouting over it, and praying for it without the revelation that in order to triumph we must first confront it.

Confronting our past and present will propel us to prepare for our future and to bless others in the process. This book is very personal but shares some divine revelations in the process. Whether Christian or other, saved or unsaved, black or white, we all have layers to discover and prayerfully this book will bless you to discover them in a productive manner that will push you forward to understand that you are not a victim but truly an overcomer and you will help others overcome by you living your authentic truth and as a result enjoying your best life. Forever the Victim? I don't think so! It's just another layer of greatness developing.

Each chapter of this book is significant to a period in my life. There is a foreword for each chapter written by an instrumental person in my life for that season. Then I continue telling you about the journey. Every chapter is closed with a divine revelation for that season and that is the thing that I learned looking back and is symbolic for the closure that I needed to complete that chapter in my life never to look back at it again.

ACKNOWLEDGEMENTS

I would like to take this time to acknowledge my family and loved ones who have helped me through this work. Thanks to my brother, my original hero, thank you for allowing me to share my truth and supporting me through this. To my family for not taking offense to the truth that was real and significant to me. To my children and my grandbaby who gave of their time with me during this process, but loved me through the dark times I had to remember to get through this process. To my life coaches thanks for being on standby. Yes, I had three professional people to see me through this craziness called my life as well as a host of Facebook family and friends. To my best friend for life, for pushing me through when I thought that I couldn't. I love you all to the moon and back.

INTRODUCTION

Here she is! The little girl that mom said she always wanted. January 11, 1975, the day that she so anxiously awaited, never knowing the responsibility that came with me, nor understanding the power of a name, she only knew that she wanted different for me than the tumultuous life she had. From what I understand she had an expectation of me before I was born. If only she knew the revelation of the words that spoke, "To whom much is given, much is required." She didn't understand that what she spoke over me were words spoken which equated to seeds being planted. The problem was that she wasn't equipped to handle the fullness of who I was, who she wanted and who God called me to be. Like the children of Israel, it took me forty years to get the revelation of this truth. Brace yourself for the road ahead called, "my life!"

I was born in Oklahoma. It seems that a child should always have a safe haven where they can always feel safe but I don't ever remember ever feeling that arc of safety except when I was in school and sometimes church. I can only recall what I remember.

I remember seeing pictures of my brother dressed in wigs because my mother was said to have this yearning for a little girl. The rest of my life, prior to my memories, was filled in by a family friend.

I was told that my mother wanted me to be the little girl she wished she could be, but she treated me like she was treated as a girl. She never told me I was pretty. I never felt like I was good enough. I never felt that I could do anything right except sing and be smart, but that was not enough. Because of these truths and experiences, even to this day, I seek affirmation and have become a shade tree but blatant overachiever.

Put your seatbelts on and get ready for this ride on the *Journey Back to Me.*

Divine Revelation

This book is in no way intended to persecute anyone. This is my truth that I walk in and live every single day. There are a number of names that have been changed for the purposes of protecting their identity but changing their name does not change my truth. I do not apologize for my experience, nor do I seek validation. This is my life and my experience told from my point of view.

1

DAUGHTER-MOM AND DAD

Chapter Foreword by (My Dad)

I thought that my proudest moment of my daughter was the day that she was born when I rushed through traffic with all lights on to witness her birth. She was my first biological child and we were bonded at conception. Our first obstacle was when the military had stationed me in Germany and I had to fight and win to get my compassion reassignment to be stationed to stay in Oklahoma until after she was born. Even though I was adopted by family members, I always knew I wanted different for my children. Even though there were limitations placed on me in reference to my access to Lolo, not by the courts, but by her mom, I was determined to be a part of her life. I knew all too well the feelings of not being able to wake up on Mother's Day and Father's Day to greet anyone and I wanted to always be there from the start to the finish of her life.

When I see, hear or think of my daughter I become even more proud. She has the same drive that I have and never achieves enough; she always seeks to expand herself. She is definitely a clone of me, from her looks to her actions. I remember watching a video of her in her office and I saw the wall behind her with all of her degrees and accomplishments, and I turned and looked at my wall and said, "Like father, like daughter."

If I had to give her any advice it would be to keep thinking forward and to continue being the best that she can be in all that she does. Most of all I want her to continue to love with passion and remember that there are a lot of things that occurred in her life that she didn't create, it was created for her and you have to love with passion to get past it.

I was so happy that despite our past Lolo asked me to give her away at her wedding and I remember the day she walked across the stage to get one of her degrees. My heart was beating with joy and love knowing that she was my child. Lolo, I love you, I am so proud of you and you will always be daddy's little girl!

The Journey Continues...

Because of the fact that my mother was a single mom, life was never easy. As a child I never remember her complaining about the struggle in all actuality, she always made life seem easy for her. I knew that my mom had a special type of hatred for my dad, but I never understood why and even to this day I still don't understand it though at times I do get an inkling. I feel now that as a child I should have never been provided that information nor her feelings, but she always made it abundantly clear how much she hated him.

I remember one time that he came to town and she made a big deal about it and threatened to have him arrested. I remember my Aunt B would always tell him whenever my brother and I would come to Texas to visit. One time she told my dad and he came to get me and my brother and took us shopping to get some clothes. Somehow my mother found out and was on the next thing smoking to come and get us and take us back. She was angry with my aunt for that reason, again I was lost. This type of behavior was typical for her and only lead to a resentful relationship between us. She made sure that she never let it be a secret how much she hated my father and how much looking at me made her sick because I looked just like him. I never knew that I had a choice.

I remember that no matter what I did, if I messed up her response was always the same, "You think that shit color is going to get you somewhere? You ain't going to be shit just like the color that you are." I wanted so bad to be dark like her and my brother so I wouldn't stand out and maybe, just maybe she would love me too like she loved my brother.

Many years later, as an adult, I found a picture of my parents. It is the only picture that I ever saw of them together. It is near and dear to my heart because it is the only sense of normalcy that I have ever seen between the two of them. I never knew that they had so many secrets between the two of them which is what caused so much resentment that neither of them explored nor expressed.

I remember one day my brother and I was having a huge fight about whose father was the best. We went round and round and finally my mom stepped in and asked what we were fighting about and I told her and I will never forget the actions that followed. The picture is still so clear in my mind to this day. It was a Saturday night, I had on my favorite orange nightgown and my hair was rolled in the old school pink rollers. My mom brought us in the living room and sat us down at her feet while she sat on the couch. She looked me in my seven year old eyes and said, "Yes, his dad is better than yours because every time we go to Texas to visit, he gives me money." I was flabbergasted to say the least. How could someone be so mean and hateful? I knew that I was wise beyond my years when my response was, "Well my daddy can't be too bad since he gave him his whole name and he is not his son." The slap that followed resounded through the universe. That day changed the fiber of my being forever.

I later found out my mother was deeply in love with my brother's father, even though they were related. Not to mention they all looked alike and as usual I was the odd ball out. This issue of discrimination in my home made my desire to meet my father even more important to me because I had so many questions in my head. Events like this happened often which made me often feel alone and neglected by my mom and they also drove a wedge between the two of us that would last a lifetime. I knew that I had to find a refuge for myself to overcome all of the bottled up feelings that I had inside of me so I turned to reading. I didn't just read normal books but I read encyclopedias and I was obsessed with the dictionary. I would be so obsessed with learning that it often got me into trouble.

Somehow, now in my adult mind, I believe that I was looking for words to articulate the pain that I was in because the words I was learning at school were inadequate to describe the magnitude of my pain and confusion. I knew at the end of the day I only wanted to be loved and accepted and this yearning would last me a lifetime.

Divine Revelation

My mother's declaration that day made me amend my desire to just have two children. Now I made my prayer more specific. I now stated that I was going to have two children and they would have the same father and we would be married forever.

SISTER

Chapter Foreword by (my brother)

I can remember it like it was yesterday, the date was January 11ᵗʰ 1975, when mom brought you home. I was so happy and thrilled! I had a baby sister, friend, and play mate. I can remember crying when people would hold you I would tell mom to tell them to put my baby down.

We have been through so much together. We had a rough start with our parents going through the stuff they were going through. There were times that I use to hate having to take you with me everywhere I went. As we grew up, I use to practice my wrestling moves on you as you got older.

As life went on we experienced so many ups and downs with mom having her set of male suitors and health problems but I tried to make sure you didn't have to see and deal with that foolishness as much as I could. This made our bond so much stronger.

The Journey Continues...

$\leftarrow\diamond\diamond\diamond\diamond\rightarrow$

All of my life I knew that my brother was loved because she always told him. See it was just me, my mom and my brother for the majority of my life, though she was married several times. I was told by my mom that she was a registered nurse and I was too young to question it. I just remember her going to work at the hospital and my brother being my primary caretaker.

I will never forget that my brother was obsessed with wrestling and so we would always watch it and I always knew that when it went off that he was going to try those moves on me. Sometimes it would be so bad that the neighbor would come and take me out of the house before my brother killed me and she would tell my mom when she got home what happened, but I never remember anything ever happening to him.

I was so young but one thing I knew is that I adored my brother. I think the adoration that I felt actually can be described as jealousy. I wanted to be more like him because I only wanted my mom to love me like she loved my brother. I knew he was her favorite, but I still wanted to believe that deep down she really did love me but perhaps she just didn't know how to show it.

Why did she hate me so??

- Could it be because she and my brother looked just alike?
- Could it be that she grew up in a house full of women and he was the male that she always longed for?
- Could it be that she really loved his father and my brother was the closest thing she had to him.

I knew that my brother loved me because he was the only consistent person in my life. While mom gambled and partied my brother was always there through hell and high water. He was the original ride or die in my life before there was such a concept. I didn't know that I would always feel a sense of responsibility to care for him for the rest of my life even though he was the oldest. I felt that it was a debt that I had to repay to him because he didn't have to love me and care for me the way he did.

My mom had a magnificent, support circle, village for us. I remember that our regular daily schedule looked like this; My big brother would get me up and get me ready for school, get himself ready, and then he would ride me on the handle bars of his bike to school until I was able to ride my own bike. This was our personal bonding time.

Never mind the fact that the ride was always the same, my brother would always make each day special in some way. Either it was a sound effect he made, or a funny story but I knew every day was going to bring something new and different and no matter what I went through and even though we fought, I knew that my brother would make it all better.

As I stated before, my brother was always my everything because he was the only consistent person in my life. No matter how different my mother tried to make us, nor how many wedges she tried to bring between us, our bond always won. Due to the relationship between my brother and me, I always knew that I wanted to have two children. As I experienced life more and more, I added additional stipulations to that desire.

Divine Revelation

Due to the care that my brother took of me, for the rest of my life I felt obligated to take care of him, even though he was the oldest. In some way, I thought that after my mother's death that she would love me more or be proud of me for taking care of her favorite child. Crazy right? Well that was my truth.

3

STUDENT- "MY FIRST REAL TEACHER"

Chapter Foreword-My Dedication to "My first real teacher"

I thank you for all that you taught me! I thank you for taking the time to get to know me as a person, not as just one of the little black girls in your class. Thank you for challenging my thinking and making me see that I mattered. If only I could tell you the hell that I was going through, but I couldn't. I didn't have the vocabulary, I didn't have the feeling, I didn't have the intellect all of which you sparked in me as a gift from the educational experience that we had. If I knew where you were, I would tell you personally how much you changed my life and how you made it worth living with your kind words and your love for children, especially me. You made me feel like I was the only child in your class. Thank you for your impartation into my life. It is thanks to your impartation that I am the educator that I am today. Thank you so much!

The Journey Continues...

My mom was not really as involved in our education as I would have liked. I never remember her going to parent-teacher conferences or any other events that took place at the school, mostly because she worked so much. The most interest that she took in me and my knowledge was when she would give my brother and I spelling bees at home. It was so interesting because she would take the dictionaries that I read on a daily basis and quiz us over words that she just knew I wouldn't be able to spell. Most of the time, our prize was five dollars. I would always win, and my brother would always get upset or cry and of course mom wouldn't like that so she would give him the prize as well. That never really mattered to me because I was just so overjoyed that she actually gave me some time and attention. This made me more and more determined to learn. Of course this love for learning spilled over into my academics at school.

I was always that kid at school who would finish my work in record timing and would be bored which forced me to seem off task. I would either begin to act out or I would just start reading books. My teachers never really knew what to do with me. This was before talented and gifted classes were implemented in schools I guess. Nevertheless, I knew now what my passion was. I loved school much more than I loved being home with my mom. School was the place that made me the happiest. Most of the greatest days of my childhood happened there. My earliest happy memory was when I was in the second grade and I remember always seeing the other kids bringing the teacher gifts as well as bringing things for show and tell. I never had anything to bring so I would take little nick nacs from the house and make up stories to tell so I would feel normal.

One year it was Christmas time and of course all of the kids were bringing something for the teacher. I just knew I wanted to bring something to "My first real teacher" because she was the first teacher that "got me." I knew that I was smart and I knew that I was bored and I would tell my mom but she didn't seem too concerned as long as I was good and didn't present any problems in class. "My first real teacher" would let me do other grade levels work so that I wouldn't cut up or cry because I was bored. I knew that I had to do something for her to show my appreciation.

I knew that I couldn't ask my mom to buy her anything or I would get cussed out so I got one of my mom's old Christian books and wrapped it in toilet paper and gave it to my teacher with a bow that I drew on it. I will never forget this experience because she seemed to overlook all of the sparkly new stuff that the other students brought and she made such a big deal out of my little raggedy book to keep the other kids from laughing at me. Never in my life had I ever felt so loved and appreciated. This was the action that made me want to be a teacher today.

My love for "My first real teacher" ran very deep; therefore, I always wanted to do things to make her happy and to help in any way that I could. She would always let me be her helper. It was nearing the end of the school year that changed my family life forever again. Yet again we had to move. Moving seemed to be a common place for us thought I never knew why.

I loved my school and I loved my teacher, to this day I still think about her, only God knows where she could be, if she is even still alive. I loved the school because the teachers became the educational village that I needed and it was there and there only that I felt safe and able to thrive. I never knew this would follow me all the days of my life.

My safety net comes in learning because it is the one thing that I do well and I can excel. Even to this day I am scared being out of school because my safety net is in the classroom. I have now taken that energy and become a student of life to try to figure it all out as best I can starting with my own healing and deliverance, no longer from people but now from myself and the chains of my past.

Divine Revelation

It is always interesting how we choose our career choice. I became a teacher because I wanted to provide the love and support that was provided to me by "My first real teacher".

13

4

IMPARTATION-MY FIRST CHURCH EXPERIENCE

Chapter Foreword-A childhood Friend

Attending church with Lolo was unforgettable. We attended church under the leadership of a preacher who had his Doctorates in Divinity and was a Master Sargent in the Army. This was a teaching church that really believed in teaching and investing in its youth. They would teach us things about order and most of the families there were military and so was the Pastor so there was not much room for error. The skills that we learned there through efforts to include Sunday School, BTU, Vacation Bible School, Girls Auxiliary and Youth Choir *are still relevant to all of your lives today. This impact is made evident in the lives and professions that we all have chosen to this day. We were all kids when we attended church together so there was not a lot to recollect since it was so long ago but one thing that I can say is that we were all like family.* I remember my grandmother being quite fond of (Lolo's Mom) and treated Lolo and her brother like her own grandchildren....

The Journey Continues...

My other place of refuge from my home life was the church. For as long as I could remember we were members of a Baptist Church in Oklahoma. I was a little girl and for as long as I could remember I would sit on the front row of the church because I just wanted to be close and never miss anything. I remember all of my "family" went to this same church and every Sunday was a treat. I would see my "cousin" Angela who led a song called, "Out on the Cross." I had a secret crush on the musicians because they could sing and play instruments. I remember the singing as well, and they all could sing so well and I remember sitting there thinking, "I want to be just like them when I get big." Little did I know I would do that and then some.

My church home was the purest form of church that I can remember. The Pastor knew all of his members. He lived in the neighborhood amongst the congregation and the church was right up the road from us. This was back in the days when the church took care of their pastor as well as each other. This set the very foundation for my love for church.

I remember right around the age of 6, I started having these dreams and I would often wonder what they meant. They varied but I would always see myself in front of people. My love for reading transitioned from the dictionary to the Bible and even as a young child, I would actually understand whatever I read. After a while I became afraid of the dreams so I told my Pastor as though he was the man to make the dreams go away but remember I had no male in my household besides my brother and I didn't think he was strong enough to handle my BIG dreams and visions. I knew in the Bible that the people went to the priest for their issues and so that is what I did.

I told my Pastor each time I had a dream and after a while he told me that I was supposed to be preaching, but I couldn't do it at the church. I saw this as another form of rejection so I began to pray and tell God to take away all of the bad men and women that wouldn't let his work be done. I had no idea what I was saying, but I now know that this was a seed planted for warfare.

It was shortly after this that I learned that "My first real teacher" had gotten sick. Then my mother began having heart issues and she was forced to not only have open heart surgery but she was also no longer allowed to work. This was when our lives changed forever.

When we got word that my mom had to have open heart surgery, I didn't really understand what that meant, but I knew that it was serious because all of my aunts and my grandmother came from Texas to Oklahoma. They tried to keep matters as normal for us as they could, but I knew something was wrong and very serious. They told my teacher what was happening. She knew that I was an above average kid so she explained to me what was going on, in a manner that I could understand. I was so confused because I didn't know what this meant for me and my brother. I sort of hoped that it meant that my brother and I would get to see my dad. Of course that didn't happen, but life was still never the same again.

They gave my mom six months to live. She could no longer work and until she recovered, she couldn't take care of us. I was more devastated that I had to leave "My first real teacher" than anything else. We went to Texas and stayed with Aunt A, my mom's older sister, for the remainder of the school year and the summer. I am assuming my mom was busy trying to regroup. This was the most normal that I ever felt.

My mother was one of six girls. Aunt A was the caretaker in the family and everyone loved her cooking. She only had two children and she was married to my uncle named Uncle D. He drunk very heavily and this caused him to always seem as though he talked funny. During this time period, Aunt A was raising her two kids, my brother and I, and two of my other cousins. No one would have ever been able to tell that we were not all her children because she treated us all the same. She made us take care and look out for one another. We stayed with her for a pretty good amount of time. It was weird because she too worked at a hospital. She was a registered nurse but she always made sure that the home front was taken care of as well. Every day she made sure that we had breakfast at home before we went to school and dinner was always ready when we got home, even though she was at work. We had a regular bath and bed time. Aunt A was amazing.

Sometimes our time was spent between the homes of Aunt A and Aunt B. Aunt B was married to Uncle R who was much older than she was. I loved Uncle R because he was really tall and very debonair. He always talked funny but somehow I could always make out what he said. I liked going to Aunt B's house only because she had the most kids so I got an opportunity to play with all my cousins. Again some kind of way she always kept in touch with my dad so she was my link to the man that I loved so dearly and longed to know so much about.

Divine Revelation

Aunt A was my superwoman. She was the woman that I wanted to be. She had two children, a boy and a girl. They had the same father and she and Uncle D were married for what seemed like forever. The most valuable lesson that she taught me was the necessity of taking care of home first and balancing that with a career.

5

STEP DAUGHTER

Chapter Foreword

As children many of us were told that when life gives you lemons to just make lemonade. We have all had some bitter lemonade that was still a little less than desirable to the taste. This fact has caused me to be more specific in my verbiage and I have purposed in my head and heart to turn my entire situation around. Yes, that thing happened to me but it does not define who I am or how I am, it was an occurrence. Yes I even did that thing more than once but guess what; it still doesn't change the great potential that God has invested in me. I purposed in my heart to make the soul choice that the sour lemons I have been given in life that I will add the sweetness of the word of God to it and the chill of experience and make some great tasty lemonade. Will you make that same choice? I hope so because life is too short to look bitter.

- 365 Revelatory Words for Any Given Day (2017)

The Journey Continues...

When my mom got better, my brother and I returned home and my mother got married to her second husband, "Clyde". He wasn't around for long and I am not sure what happened between them. My only memory was of him explaining the concept of "a couple".

My mom told me that I could have a couple of cookies and I went and got a handful of them. "Clyde" came in the kitchen and reminded me that I was only to get "a couple" of cookies and not the handful that I had. I asked him, "Well what is a couple?" He said, "Your mom and I are a couple, so how many people are we?" I said, "Two" and he said that is what a couple is." He was gone a few days later and we never saw him again. Talk about a short season and a precise purpose.

Shortly after that, my mom met the man that I will forever consider my dad, "Bob". The two people above were the main factors in my life. They were together for some of the most tumultuous times in my life and they also left some of the most impacting impressions on my life, more than I was able to admit. My dad, "Bob", was the man that showed me what manhood was. I know that my mom took him through some changes but he still tried to love her past all of that for many years. My mother had a gambling addiction that nearly cost him everything but I had no clue how bad it was until we got to Germany.

This man and I were like two peas in a pod. He was literally my everything for a number of years. I am not sure how long they dated, but he was in the military and he got orders to go to Europe. He and mom had an on again and off again relationship. I am thinking that they were in an off state when he came over to our apartment that we lived in and woke us up in the middle of the night to ask us permission to marry our mom. I couldn't be more excited. "Bob" was a Capricorn just like me. His birthday was two days after mine. He was responsible, caring and gentle. He had a daughter named "Bob"ine, but she lived with her mom in California and in some ways I am thinking we were so close because I was the daughter that he was missing. As soon as they got married, they bought this huge house in Oklahoma and then we were ordered by the military to move to Europe. This is where my life began to get super interesting.

Divine Revelation

Sometimes in life transition can become a dichotomy to the life of an individual. Not only are you changing physical location, but also the mental space that you are in can be transformed as well. That transformation can be a positive or a negative but whatever the transformation, it can and will shift your being as well.

6

MILITARY BRAT-EUROPE

Chapter Foreword by (my brother)

When we moved to Europe I thought that it would make matters better but it brought on a new set of challenges, from you being raped, to people using you to get to me.

In addition to seeing what life was like outside the United States, this chapter made me start to see you grow and mature. It also gave me a glimpse into your health issues with the seizures and depression that you were experiencing. I had no idea of what you were going through, but all this made me lose fake friends and put my guards up to try to prevent any more hurt and harm to come your way.

The Journey Continues...

We arrived in Europe and I was a big ball of emotions and feelings. I had never been out of the states of Texas and Oklahoma so surely I didn't know what to expect outside the country. Little did I know that this experience would change the very fiber of my being.

I remember we lived in housing and my mom had a home daycare where she cared for small children for the military soldiers in our housing complex. She would watch them in the day while they worked and they would hire me to watch them at night because mom's hours didn't extend beyond the start time of Bingo. I thought this was a great opportunity for me to make some money, if only my mom wouldn't take it away from me.

I loved when my mom had her daycare because it was the closest that I had to a regular childhood like what we had at Aunt A's house. My mom had a snack for me afterschool and dinner would even often times be ready by the time I came home. It was great! Even more than that, it was like I had little sisters and brothers around the house to play with and have fun like kids were supposed to. This happiness was short lived because her addiction got the best of her. My mom would make my brother and I go and cash hot checks for her so that she could go and play bingo. My brother got caught stealing at the local market and worst of all my life changed forever during this time.

We would still go to church and my mom would often let me and my brother go to the local pizzeria and eat as hush incentives when she would lie and say she was going to church when really she was going to bingo. I loved their Calzones and she knew how to make me happy and how to make me hush. I would either love being in church or at the pizza bar. This all worked out well until a time came where there was nowhere for me to go. It was a Monday night and there was no church and the pizza bar was

24

not open but she had to go and play bingo and I was not old enough to go in. She took my brother, but left me.

In our housing, there was a basement where there were storages and a laundry room. She told me to stay home, go down to the cellar, and wait until she and my brother got back. I did just that, I got a dictionary, which was my favorite read, and I went to the cellar. I was down there for what seemed like forever, then my brother's best friend "The Predator" came through. It was not unusual for the kids in the neighborhood to play in the basement. It just wasn't my thing; I would rather read or do something academic, after all "My first real teacher" told me that I was considered a talented and gifted kid. Little did I know that this cellar would become the closet that I would metaphorically stay trapped in for a good portion of my life.

I sat down there and practiced for my upcoming spelling bee when "The Predator" came and began talking to me. Nothing unusual, he was always quite friendly to me. He was the first cross eyed person I had ever met, so I found him quite intriguing. Then the moment came where our conversation turned "nasty". He was talking to me about stuff I had never heard of because I was in elementary school and I was so into my studies and church that everything else seemed foreign to me. Before I knew it he was taking full advantage of me sexually. Yes, he raped me! I bled profusely from the fight and I didn't know what else to do but run upstairs and tell my dad. "Bob" was shocked and livid. His first question was, "Where is your mama?" I knew that I would get in trouble if I told so I just said, "I didn't know!" He immediately knew where she was. It seemed like right then and there she walked through the door and began fussing at me saying how she had been looking for me for hours.

My dad saw right through it and pulled my mom in the bedroom and told her what had happened. Would you believe she said, "That bitch is lying and she probably gave it away and I'm not taking her nowhere!" I was hurting, embarrassed and felt so super dirty. My brother overheard the conversation and told my parents that he was taking the dog for a walk. The few minutes between these occurrences seemed like forever. The impact of me bleeding everywhere, my mom and dad found it to be the time to fight over fault and my brother wanted to take matters into his own hands and walk the dog and where was I, sitting there alone, hurting, feeling abandoned because I was alone, feeling guilty for telling and getting my mom in trouble, hurting from the act and unsure of what would happen from this point on. My dad rushed me to the hospital and got me taken care of while my mom and brother stayed home.

Time went by and I felt like my mother and I had a relationship that will never be the same. Not that it was so great to begin with, but now it was worse than it had ever been. The babysitting gigs became more frequent and I felt like my mom was doing it to keep me out of the house. I swear I felt like she told all of her clients about what happened which made them cling closer to me and embrace me. There was one family that I worked for that I loved their little girl name Yolanda because she looked a little like me, she was just a little chunky.

I baby sat her on the regular because her parents couldn't get along. Her dad was huge and very abusive to her mom, but he was always nice to me then of course I found out why, he too took advantage of me. I knew I couldn't say anything to my parents about this because the last time, it tore my family apart and my mother never let me live it down. She reminded me nearly daily how stupid I was and how worthless I was. I kept this one to myself. This went on for some time because my mom still didn't want me home, my brother was doing his own thing and my dad worked a lot. I felt stuck and I felt like this was all I was good for.

Divine Revelation

***Needless to say this little girl never knew her worth, nor
did she think she was worth exploring it because surely
it would be garbage. That is how she felt and that is how
she perceived herself but the saga only continues.***

7

FRIEND TO THE FRIENDLESS-USING ME TO GET TO MY BROTHER

Chapter Foreword by (my brother)

You tried to tell me how people would use you to be my friend while we were in Germany. I didn't notice it. However, when the time came for us to return to the states, we moved to Georgia. I thought the new location would bring about new beginning, but when we get there, more harsh realities come to light.

I was a senior in high school and you were in middle school and that's when I personally saw people claiming to be your friends, but were actually just using you to get to me again. We found some solitude in joining church. We started singing with the young adult choir. That gave us an outlet. I was then made aware of you being taunted by our mom to be more like me.

The Journey Continues...

I had one good friend named "Miesha". She was older than I was and my mom didn't really like me hanging out with her because of that. We were always together though; I really thought that she wanted to be my friend. I later found out that she only wanted to be my friend because she liked my brother. This too became a commonplace. Girls were crazy about my brother because he was a tall, black, berry that knew the right things to say and do to make girls melt, even to this day. I never understood it, probably because he is my brother, but this behavior continued on for many years.

As a result of what I went through I found myself wanting to attend church even the more. I didn't learn much from the sermons because I couldn't understand them with all of the whooping and hollering, but I do remember the music and it became my life. I remember that there were some pivotal people in our music department that I would never forget.

"Aretha" was one of those people. She was in the adult choir and she sang like it was no one's business. Her signature song was, "Don't Wait til the Battle Is Over, Shout Now!" I so wanted to believe what she was saying, but I didn't know how to shout and I didn't see a reason to shout. My home life was horrible. I always felt like an inconvenience, like I was in the way. My brother who was always my savior was doing his own thing. I was forced to babysit this little girl who I loved but her dad would put her to sleep before I arrived and "have his way with me" until it was almost time for his wife to come home from work. What could I possibly shout about?

"Marty" was my second favorite singer. He was in the children's choir with me. The only difference was that I hated the children's choir. I hated it so bad that I would get in trouble for not singing out and always holding my head to the side. If only they would have taken the time to explore why

I really felt the way I felt. Marty's signature song was, *"Take Me Back."* The lyrics of this song are,

> *"Take me back, take me back dear Lord,*
> *to the place where I first received you.*
> *Take me back; take me back dear Lord where I first believed."*

This song was my life. It spoke to my exact situation. I wanted to go back home to Oklahoma where I felt safe. Where my brother and I were together and life was easier and I felt normal but that was not an option.

Finally, there was "Freddy!" He was like a big brother to me. He was in the adult choir as well. This man sang like his life depended on it. His signature song was *"In Times like these."*

> *In times like these, we need a Savior*
> *In times like these, we need a Savior*
> *Be very sure, be very sure*
> *Your anchor holds and grips the Solid Rock.*

I am sharing the lyrics to these songs, because these are the songs that got me through one of the first dark times of my life.

For the duration of my life I have always sought to explore, who I was, my importance and what it is that I could do well. The only thing that really brought me joy was church and school. After all, these were my only safe places. These were the places that I could escape the pain of the repeated molestation, the ridicule of my brother, who now seemed to have turned on me, the hatred of my mom and the insecurities that I held within. It wasn't long before we went back to the States and man did my life change tremendously yet again.

After years of being in Europe, it was time to go back to the U.S. I was so excited. I would do anything to get back to Oklahoma. I began to blossom. I remember my sixth grade graduation from the schools in Germany; I had even mustered up enough courage to sing a solo in front of the whole school. I didn't tell my mom or my brother because I felt that they would just make fun of me or tell me that I couldn't do it so I decided to lean on the support of my teachers. They were so awesome.

I remember that they reminded me of "My first real teacher". I would always get caught singing in the bathroom at school and finally one day I began singing songs by this great lady named Whitney Houston. I was so creative I would stand in the mirror and sing it in English and in German. I guess that's where my overachieving personality began.

I remember that at school the word on the street was that they wanted to make this graduation a year to remember because two of my teachers were retiring. Ms. B which was the only teacher of color I had ever seen. She taught us Geography. She was the first person in my entire life to tell me that I could travel the world internationally. She showed me a globe and told me that I could reach every person in every continent. This was inconceivable for me. She told me that I could be the next Whitney Houston. "Do you think that we teachers don't know about your gift?" She asked.

Gift? What is that? I had no clue what she was talking about, I didn't have any presents. What on earth could she mean? I really wanted to know about this gift she spoke of but I didn't want to tell her I didn't know what she meant for fear of sounding stupid.

One day I had made up a song to help me remember the continents and the countries in Europe. I shared the song with her and then she made me sing the song in front of my class. I wasn't scared because school was my "safe place." The other teachers heard me singing and then they started announcing for auditions for someone to sing for graduation. I never gave it a thought.

Then Ms. B told me that she needed to see me at lunch. I had no idea what she wanted but I went as I was told. When I got there, there were a number of teachers there and my heart sank. I thought, "Oh my goodness, I have really done it this time!" The teachers were all looking at me and smiling so now I was confused. All at once, I envisioned "My first real teacher" and thought, "All teachers are nice and they are your friends."

Finally, Mr. R spoke and said, "Lolo, we have all been talking and we have all heard you sing and would like for you to try out for the singing at the graduation." I thought I had peed my pants!

Are you serious? You don't know my life! I have nothing to sing about! My mom hates me; my brother makes fun of me. My dad is always in the field and I am made to go babysit this little girl and take care of this man's wife's duties. How could I sing? What would I sing? I had a million and one questions in my head and they were all trying to come out at once, but I had vowed to myself that I would never tell about the molestation. I loved my family too much to say anything so I just looked with a blank stare. Before I knew it a tear fell out of my eye and all of the teachers in the room embraced me and told me that I could do it. They asked me to sing Whitney Houston's "Greatest Love of All."

I loved the song and the artist but I didn't think I had the confidence to sing it, especially in front of people. They gave me a copy of the lyrics and I had to read them over and over. Every day at lunch, I got to eat lunch with the teachers and they would prep me for my performance. Somehow, we evolved from auditioning to preparing. I didn't care I enjoyed the quality time amongst people that I felt loved and cared for me. I told them that I wanted to surprise my mom and that I didn't want them to call her and they agreed. I practiced and practiced and practiced.

Finally the day came and I was a nervous wreck. They had my name on the program and all. I just hoped my mom didn't read it. It seemed like the rest of the program was a blur. Finally the moment of truth came. They talked about me and gave a brief introduction of how I came to be chosen to sing at the graduation. I couldn't do it. I didn't want to look in my mom's face. I couldn't help but wonder in my mind, was she happy? Was she proud? Was she angry? Would she embarrass me? Well here comes the moment. Mr. R called my name and told me to come up. My feet felt glued to the floor and my butt felt glued to the seat. Somehow I mustered up enough strength to take that long dreadful 50 ft. walk to the stage. I got to the podium and I done as my teachers trained me. Imagine the audience is full of your favorite people, favorite food and/or that no one is there but you. I did all of the above. I imagined all of my teachers, especially "My first real teacher", were sitting in the audience eating pork chops and macaroni and cheese. I couldn't help but notice my mom who had ran to the front of the auditorium and was taking pictures with the biggest smile on her face I had ever seen.

Suddenly the music started and it was sink or swim time. My mouth got dry, my hands got wet. What if I forget my words? What if nothing comes out? Oh Lord, why me? Finally I got my musical cue and I closed my eyes and began singing. Wow! It was amazing and before I knew it the song was over. I think I found a new favorite place, on stage. I opened my eyes! My mom was crying and gleaming with joy. "Bob" was standing next to my seat clapping with amazement. I got a standing ovation. My classmates were cheering, the teachers were crying and finally I made my way off stage with a line of people ready to hug me and congratulate me. It was at that moment that I realized I could sing.

From that moment on I became addicted to the stage. The stage became my friend and finally people wanted to be my friend because I was in the spotlight. A clear preemption of what was to come though I had no idea. I didn't realize it then, but I realize it now that I exchanged my friendless state to becoming a friend because people wanted to be with my brother to becoming a friend because I was a fad. In others eyes, I was a small celebrity. I wish I could say I embraced the attention but I didn't. Inside I was torn with my worth, the sexual abuse, and the changes taking place in my body which I didn't understand and just trying to find my place in the world.

Divine Revelation

Because I lived so many years in relationships where people only wanted to be next to me for an ulterior motive, I secluded to a personal cave every time I encountered someone, and I found safety in being alone but this is only after I entered into relationships giving all I got because I wanted people to find me valuable.

Victim to Victim-Rape to Promiscuity

Chapter Foreword

How many storms have we all gone through where we felt as though we couldn't and wouldn't tell anyone what was going on. We held that storm dear to our hearts for fear of ridicule and shame and of course judgment. There are all types of storms that we choose to keep a secret so we paste on the phony smiles on our faces and we put on our hallelujah hats and we dance all over the storm only to return to it in our own private time. This is where the spiritual and emotional roller coaster comes in and it only opens the door for other issues to manifest and in turn you keep those a secret as well and before you know it you are living a lie and in a secret world of deceit. From the place no good thing can be birthed but more and more issues. The first thing to understand is that you cannot hide anything from God and ultimately he is the one to share it with and more importantly he is the only one that can do something about it. Just be honest and allow him into your secret storm and watch him work it out.

- 365 Revelatory Words for Any Given Day (2017)

The Journey Continues...

We are now back into the states in the great state of Georgia. My perception of myself was still worthless and I felt that my only value was my vagina. This belief continued though my teenage years. I began dressing inappropriate for my age. I began singing secular music; anything with sex in it. I began hanging around my brother and his friends, even if it was from afar because I knew what it took to get their attention and I did it all, from playing cheerleader as they played basketball to changing clothes when I got to school. I didn't do this while we were in Europe because I was being sexed enough at my babysitting job, however, when we got back to the states, I realized that I had become used to being sexually active so I started seeking sexual attention again.

This is the reason why I call this chapter victim to victim because I didn't know how to break this cycle and for me it became a new normal. I would always want to play house though I was well past that age, and then I wanted to be the mom and I would lock myself up with the person playing the dad and….need I say more. I tried so hard to contain myself but I didn't know how. Little did I know that this is where my sex addiction stemmed from. The manifestation would soon take over in more ways than one.

Soon after arriving in Georgia, I would begin hanging out in the neighborhood and I was giving myself to boys and neither of us knew what we were doing. I took a lot of virginities because I felt like I was a sex connoisseur. I knew exactly what to do and when to do it. I could tell the boys when they were about to cum and when to pull out. I had missionary down pat and was ready to start experimenting with new positions so I became attracted to older guys who I thought could teach me something and I didn't have to be the bedroom boss anymore. No one had a clue as to what I was doing. My brother was doing his own thing and my parents were having marital issues so I was left to my own devices, destruction.

Divine Revelation

It is always said that hindsight is 20/20. As I began writing this book, I couldn't help but cry at the truth that I never noticed. I never realized how much sex was a big part of who I was and for the longest time, I allowed it to define me and change the elements of my life that meant the most to me. It took many years to get over the aftershocks of a few moments of pleasure. Sex changes the most in-depth parts of who you are especially when you exposed to it before you can intellectually, mentally and emotionally process it. It's not just a physical act.

9

COMPANION TO THE ABANDONED-
MY BROTHER LEFT FOR COLLEGE

Chapter Foreword

Have you ever experienced the abandonment of people in your life? Have you ever been disappointed by their ability to just walk away when you felt like you needed them the most? Here is the great revelation of this matter, if they were meant to stay, they couldn't leave. By virtue of the fact that they are able to leave means that God never intended for them to stay in the first place. It's a hard pill to swallow but it is the truth. If you chase them and make them stay, they will only block or maybe delay the blessings that are coming your way. Keeping people in your life beyond their expiration date will only bring spoilage to you harvest. Let them go and watch you grow!

- 365 Revelatory Words for Any Given Day (2017)

The Journey Continues...

We had just gotten back to the states so we were in a small trailer awaiting my parents to find a house. Things had gotten really bad between my mom and "Bob" and he had become abusive to her. I remember the first time I saw him strike her, I was mortified.

It was Saturday and we knew that before any playing or hanging out took place we had to do our chores. My brother and I had just come in from taking the garbage out. The chores were done so now all we had to do was go to the laundry mat. My brother was in the shower and I heard mom and dad in the living room shouting at each other. The next thing I know I heard bangs and some tussling going on. I rushed out of my room only to find my mom pinned down on the couch and her head was bleeding.

All I saw was the blood and I began screaming. My brother came rushing out of the shower, by this time "Bob" was throwing my mom onto my bed. I was a nervous wreck! My brother came out asking questions and I was too shaken up to answer anything. Finally, he began cleaning my mom up and told me to calm down. He had now become my superman again and my respect for him sky rocketed.

My mom told us to gather the laundry so that we could go to the laundry mat. I was torn. I mean I didn't have a wonderful relationship with my mom but I never wanted to see her hurt either. I didn't want to go to the laundry mat because I was afraid of what might happen to her but she insisted that she would be fine. From that moment on I was now terrified of the man that I once adored.

My brother and I went to the laundry mat and I was still weeping and afraid, though my parents were acting as though nothing happened and it seems as though my brother was too, I was still scared. Did I miss something? What just happened here? Did anyone besides me notice the injury to my mother's head? Ok, well let's just act like nothing happened then.

Moving forward, we finally moved into our house and I thought we were going back to being normal again. It was time for my brother to graduate high school. I will never forget that we had distant family come to Georgia to visit us. It was my "cousin" and some other people, I don't remember who all came but I just remember them telling my brother that they were coming back to get him after he graduated and that they would see to it that he went to college back in Oklahoma where they were from.

I was devastated at the thought. My mom and dad were fighting more often; I was sexually frustrated because I was really trying to turn my life around. I no longer had the stage and spotlight and now my brother was getting ready to leave me! What was I supposed to do? Where was I supposed to go? How was I to survive without my lifeline?

I knew that in my life there were two people in my life that meant more to me than life itself, "Bob" and my brother. Don't get me wrong, I loved my mom too but there was a wall in our relationship that I could not get past. I loved those two guys more than anything and even though "Bob" was abusive towards my mom, I knew that he loved me and he was the only man who ever loved me in the purest form of love. Now we were at a crossroads.

The loves of my life were leaving me. My brother left for college and I didn't know how to cope. I threw myself into church like never before. I would catch the church bus to and from church because my mom would only go sometimes. I began taking babysitting gigs again because I didn't want to be home. I started babysitting for some of the families in our church and guess what; there was another dad who found me "interesting." Now he didn't go as far as the other dad did, but he would sure kiss me each time he picked me up from my house. He was the drummer at our church and his wife was one of the deaconesses. This just added to the confusion that was my life.

There was so much going on in my life right now. Mom and dad were fighting awfully now, my brother was gone and I was left to deal with it all on my own. I remember one day they got into a fight and again I was in my room doing my homework and I heard the tussling again. This time I heard my mom begging him to stop, so I ran in the living room and I saw my mother laying on the track of the patio door and my dad was closing the door on her head. ENOUGH WAS ENOUGH! I ran and got a lamp and threw it. I was furious and I had had enough. I was just a little girl barely 5 feet tall and barely 100 pounds compared to my brother's 6 foot frame, but I knew that I was fed up with the fighting. "Bob" came after me but I took off to my room and tried to call the police, but he had ripped the phone out of the wall. Mom begged and pleaded with me not to come out and not to do anything "stupid". What did that mean? Now I was really confused. I thought I was protecting her. Lord, could life get any more confusing for me? Of course it could!

The next Sunday, my mom didn't go to church because she was still nursing her wounds. I remember we had a long day. We had Sunday School, Morning Service and then we had a musical that evening and I needed all the help I could get so I asked them could I stay all day. They both agreed. I was a kid in a candy store. I stayed for all services. At the musical there were groups from all over there, and in one of the groups was our family friend "Freddy" from Germany. I was so excited, and he sounded great. I thought that my parents would be just as excited to see him as I was so I let him take me home instead of me catching the church bus. I got home and rushed through the door with excitement and I told my parents who brought me home. They didn't seem as thrilled as I was. They were cordial to him. As soon as he left, they told me to go clean the kitchen.

I was still a little confused as to the cold reception. I went in the kitchen and began cleaning. All of a sudden "Bob" came into the kitchen and slapped me around a bit. I was so confused as to why I was being beaten like this. He didn't even warn me or say anything so now I was even more confused. As if his slapping me around wasn't enough, now here comes my mom! She thought the slapping was too rational so she started punching me. One lick, two licks, three licks, four! She grabbed me by my hair and banged my head on the counter and then she drug me by my hair into the laundry room and began banging my head on the edge of the washer. I had never felt so much excruciating pain in my life up to that point. I still had no idea why I got beat so bad.

Finally "Bob" came back in and asked me, "Who told you to catch a ride home with Freddy?" I thought to myself, "Is that what all this was about? …A ride from church with a family friend?" I remember cleaning the kitchen and taking my monstrous headache to bed. I was hurting too bad to even shower. I was feeling dizzy and completely discombobulated, but I had to pull myself together to go to school the next day.

When I got to school the next day, middle school mind you, all of my teachers kept asking me what was wrong. I didn't want to tell them, I just cried and cried and cried. Finally, my school house love interest "teacher" knew something was wrong and he sent me to the office. I went to the counselor and told them what happened. I begged them not to call my parents, but what was the first thing they did? They called my mom.

I don't know if I have mentioned it up to this point, but my mom was an Oscar worthy actress. The counselor was talking to my mom and my mom began telling her all about her heart issues and all of this and that. She even blamed the bruises on her from "Bob" on me. Before I knew it I was the villain. This was a painful reminder of Germany, when I told and I became the villain, and now this. That's it! I'm not telling anybody else anything, I don't care what it is!

I remember they called my dad back from NTC which is the National Training Center for the Military to prepare for battle. This was synonymous of what I was going through. He came home and he and my mom had a conversation. I went straight to my room and laid down. I wasn't sure which hurt most, the hurt in my head or my heart. Again I had told the truth and it turned around and was made to be my fault.

I remember my parents making me get up and sit on the patio for a moment. I didn't know what was happening but half of me didn't even care anymore. It is what it is! After what seemed like an eternity of sitting in the sunlight with what I know now to be a concussion, they finally came and got me. They told me to come and get in the car that we were going for a ride. I remember hearing my mom say she needed a break. I had no idea what that meant, but I felt the same way. I didn't mean the type of break I am about to tell you about though.

Divine Revelation

When a child tells the truth and always seems to get scrutinized for telling the truth, it is planting a seed of silence. As you can

see so far in the book that every time I told a truth, I was further victimized in it by being called a liar. This makes the truth a numbing place, a place that I would shy away from. For many reasons now I could see how and why habitual liars become the way they are. It doesn't make it right, but it does make it understandable. Sometimes the truth is just too painful.

10

DESERTED AND DESOLATE- THE MENTAL HOSPITAL

Chapter Foreword by (my brother)

I didn't believe you when you told me that our stepfather was abusing mom until I saw it for myself. I hated to leave for college because I knew it meant leaving you alone to fight by yourself. When I was away I heard that you had been committed to the mental hospital and that you had attempted suicide.

The Journey Continues...

——————◆◆◆◆◆——————

We got into the car and began to ride. I noticed that we were passing everything that was familiar to me. I saw the interstate; I just knew that we were going on a vacation. "Bob" was good for surprising us with road trips. This road trip felt so different. Inside, there was something gnawing at me to let me know that things would never be the same again, but I didn't know how or what this feeling meant. After a little over an hour, we pulled up to this place that looked like a huge resort. I was so excited even in the midst of my pain.

My mom and dad got out and told me to stay in the car and that they would be right back. This wasn't uncommon; it is what they did whenever they went to check into a hotel. This time still seemed different. The gnawing wouldn't stop. Finally, after an eternity in the car in the hot beaming sun, I saw my mom and dad coming out with these two big guys in white uniforms.

My heart began beating so fast I could feel it in my throat. My hands began to sweat and then they began to tremble. The hairs on my neck began to stand up and I got goose bumps. Finally, they made it to the car. They told me to get out but I couldn't. My butt felt like steel that was pushing against the cushion of the seat. My body became limp as though I had no control of it but it also felt heavy and as though it weighed a ton. I guess they took it as though I was being defiant and the big guys began to pull me out of the car.

As any child would, I began crying out to my mom for help! "Help Mommy please!!" I cried! "I promise I will be good and I will never tell anything again!" "You can do whatever and I will never say another word!"

As I tried to fight these big men off, I remember catching a glance of my mom's face with a lifetime movie smirk on her face. She never said anything, but the look on her face spoke volumes. "Finally, I get rid of her!" "Finally, I can be free again!"

I looked over to "Bob", the last heartbeat that I had and he had tears in his eyes and had walked away. I could only imagine what he was thinking. He knew everything that I had already been through in my little life and now this.

Initially I wasn't being defiant but after a while I felt like I was the only hope I had left. No one was there to protect me so I had to do it myself. I began fighting these bad men back. I gave one a punch to the nuts and the one I bit as I tried to run away. I had really done it this time. They called for backup and they put me in physical restraints. I never lost my fight though, I was determined to get away and to get answers as to why I was being put through this. I knew I hadn't done anything wrong but just be born. I never asked for that either. In an instant I became mad at the world. I was even mad at God and I didn't care who knew it. As I fought these men off, my life was flashing before me and all that I had went through. I was no longer just fighting these men; I was fighting the boy who raped me, the men who molested me. I was even fighting the other men and boys I had been with even though it was consensual. I was mad as hell and I wanted the world to know it.

Before I knew it they had me in a strait jacket and tied me to a stretcher. It still didn't calm me all the way down, so they sedated me. For a brief moment, I thought I had won even though I was still in restraints. In my little twelve year old mind, I thought I had been vindicated. Then I saw that they rolled me into a padded room. My body was too limp to do anything, or so I thought. They took me off the stretcher as I began dozing off. I thought the battle was over until they placed me on another bed and tried to tie me down again. This time I wasn't having it. I felt like the girl in the exorcist. It was time to fight back. Fight back for the little girl's innocence that was stolen at such a young age. Fight back for the kid who was consistently ignored and abandoned by her parents. There was a rage inside of me that had to come out and this was my opportunity to fight back in my own way and say, "ENOUGH IS ENOUGH!"

They tied me to this bed but the rage in me was so strong that I yanked the bolted bed from the floor and flipped the bed over on top of myself. I remember the guy looking at me and saying, "That's what you get!" After he said that, he left me there. It wasn't long until the paramedics came to tend to my wounds. I was so angry that everything I saw was red. I took that to mean that I was out for blood. The paramedic looked at the bolted bed on top of me and stood in awe and amazement that a child with such a small frame could do such damage. Little did they know I felt as though I was fighting for my life and the liberation that I could not articulate, but so desperately longed for.

She was so nice to me as she tended to my wounds. She asked me the question, "Where does all that strength come from that you can rip a bolt out of cement?" My only response to everything was, "I'm so tired! I give up!" She looked me in my face and said, "Never say those words again! From this you shall draw strength, more strength than the strongest super hero that you can imagine!" My reply was, "I don't want to be a superhero, and I just want to be super loved!" She looked in my eyes and let out the biggest sigh and I felt like she was breathing a sigh of relief just for me.

I stayed in solitary confinement for the night. I had to sleep all of the sedation off. The next day, I met with my therapist. He was a goofy looking white man, I don't remember his name. He gave me a battery of assessments only to determine that I was not crazy, but had been abused and set up. He filled me in as to where I was. It was a mental hospital in Georgia. I was there because my mother had told them that I abused her. "WHAT???" "Yes," he said, "she stated that the bruises and all that she had came from you!"

"You have got to be kidding me? What about my bruises and wounds?"

"She said she did that in self-defense."

"Here is how this goes Lolo," the doctor stated, "How long you are in here is determined by you and your behavior."

I looked in complete disbelief as to the words that I was hearing right now. "How I behave?" All I ever did was try to defend her and do my best to love her and make her proud of me. How could this be happening to me?

The doctor continued on saying, "You will be in therapy three times a week. You will attend group meetings the other four days and in addition to all of this, you will also have family therapy sessions where your mom and dad come to the therapy sessions as well."

I thought to myself, "This cannot be happening and of course, no good can come from this but hey what choice do I have."

I wind up being in there the entire summer. During that summer I had two roommates commit suicide. We had several breakout attempts and lock downs. Every family session turned out to be a circus act that my mom performed and played the innocent victim.

I felt like this was my time to tell all. I told everything from the rape to the abuse. I told about how my mother used to call me in from outside to come and bring her a glass of water. How she used to make us run her bathwater and I was made to bathe in her dirty bathwater. I felt like this was my only chance to tell what was happening that I never had the chance or the courage to tell before, besides, I didn't know who to tell.

They even reached out to my brother to confirm my allegations and guess what? He said none of this ever happened. I was baffled! I couldn't believe my eyes or ears. How could he? Again I felt betrayed by yet another heartbeat. This made me go to a special kind place of shut down. I made up in my mind I never wanted to see him again. I hated everything about him and my mom; I detested the very existence of my dad ("Bob") because though he tried to help me, my mom threatened to go to his commanding officer with the abuse allegations which would ultimately get him put out of the military.

Prior to me being released to go home, I had to do home visits on the weekend. I was coming to hate those times too. All I did was cook and clean and be the slave that I was in the beginning. Then I get there and realize that "Bob"ine, "Bob's daughter, was there for the summer and was sleeping in my room and guess what? I was made to clean up behind her as well. Slowly I was beginning to see why my friends at the hospital were killing themselves. It crossed my mind several times. Like a dummy I told my therapist and they began putting me on suicide watch every time I came back.

The more time I spent in this place the closer I became to the people that worked there as well as the other patients. We knew we were all we had. It seemed as though it was us against the world. This hospital became our world and our reality. We were the family that none of us really had.

When it became time to go, only because my insurance had ran out. This was the most somber day ever, or so I thought.

When I got home, it wasn't long before my mom and "Bob" were separating and later divorced.

Divine Revelation

This message is for all the people who are reading this book that tried to tell about some abuse or misfortune that they experienced. It is your experience and you do not have to seek approval nor validation to tell your truth. It is your truth and your experience. Tell it and tell it again and you keep telling it until the enemy can no longer hold you hostage to it. Remember that each time that you don't tell it, there is another brick added to the protective wall that you don't even realize that you are living behind. Tell!

11

To Fill a Void- "Derrick" and My daughter

Chapter Foreword by (my brother)

I came home to visit and we would spend time as I see you are growing in the beautiful woman I knew you would become. However, mom's taunting sent you looking for love in the wrong places. I remember calling home to hear you crying, afraid to tell me that you had gotten pregnant with your daughter and now life takes you on a whole new road. You were 16 with a child and having to not only worry about yourself, but also a child.

As if that wasn't enough, that heartbreaking day comes when our mom passes now leaving you truly alone in the world. Still, you endured the struggle and came out stronger. We had two funerals that took a lot out of you so you didn't attend the second which you were ridiculed for by our family.

Despite all odds, you still finished school even though the world said that you would be another statistic but you proved them all wrong.

As time goes by and I come to visit only to see that you are having to deal with the lack of a solid foundation of a happy home with "Derrick" and his job situations. I remember him being jealous that I was helping you with the baby.

You always wondered why I didn't like him. It was because of the day he came to your house when you all were separated and took the baby and after the

LOLO

tussle of you fighting for your child, he left you passed out on the ground after you had a seizure.

Sadly, you was in love and took him back and later had a second child. I applaud you that despite the difficulties, you yet still endured and pressed on.

The Journey Continues...

—◆◇◆◇◆—

After my mom and "Bob" divorced I was forced to live alone with her. I knew that no good thing could come of that. I was not just angry; I was enraged by the entire situation. I had trust issues. I had love issues. I still battled with sex issues. I was a broken vessel and I just wanted to be loved authentically and not judged for my past.

I did everything that I could to show my rage within reason. I became a bully at school. I would go in my room and perform in front of the mirror because I still felt the pull of God but "outside of his presence" I was a terrorist. I went on to date a number of boys, at one time I even dated two brothers. One was a student with me and the other was a grown man. I got with some of my friends and we went to the barracks of Fort Stewart which is where all of the single military men lived and we were into all types of mischief.

Finally I met the brother of one of my friends that I was a bully with at school. Her parents were away for the weekend and I pulled the old trick and told my mom her parents were there. When my mom went to drop me off, he opened the door and I heard angels, or so I thought. He was tall, dark, and handsome, he had pretty teeth, and I loved everything about him.

The weekend began and I was all over him. He was older than me and had been a tad bit more experienced then I was. He was the first man to ever perform oral sex on me. I thought He and I had died and went to heaven. I was hooked. His mom was the pianist at the same church my mom went to. It didn't take long for he and I to become an item. Little did I know I was using him to replace the void of one of my heartbeats.

We did everything together. We were inseparable. I was able to be myself around him and he felt the same way. I knew that I felt half complete when I was with him. It was the first time that I felt ready to start a family, even though I was only fifteen. I told him of my desire and he was down for it so we started working on it. We were sexing all the time trying hard to work on this baby that we both wanted so bad. It was our little secret.

Months went on and finally I became pregnant. I was the happiest girl alive until the sickness started to kick in and I could not keep up with my changing body. I went to the free clinic and found out that I was pregnant for sure. Yes, I forged the paperwork to be seen and all but nevertheless, I got the assurance I needed. "Derrick" had to work so I had to walk home from the clinic. I remember thinking how different my life was going to be. I had a long conversation with the baby inside of me and told it how we were going to be okay and that I was going to do everything in my power to make sure that my baby knew that he or she was loved. A short lived love affair it was.

I finally got the courage to tell my mom and when I did she beat me. Blow by blow I felt it necessary to do whatever I could to protect my baby. Finally, the beating became too intense and I couldn't do anything but take it. Inside I feared that if I fought her back that she would then send me back to the mental hospital, so I took it. When she was done I was in so much pain. I never told "Derrick" or anyone else until I woke up in the middle of the night bleeding. Oh my goodness! It hurt so badly. I thought my period was just coming but this was a new kind of pain beyond my normal debilitative menstrual cramps. I called "Derrick" and told him and he took me to the Army hospital. They told me I had to get my mother's consent to be treated. I wouldn't dare call her so I called her best friend in hopes that she would work good enough. Epic fail! They had to call my mom anyways. I was mortified. I never told them what happened to me, but it didn't take long for them to piece it together. My mom had beaten me until I had a miscarriage. I had a miscarriage at the age of fifteen.

I was angry. I was livid. I felt the need to get revenge for my baby's sake. Not that it would bring my baby back, but that was the closest I had ever felt to being loved and authentically connected to something or someone. I loved "Derrick" and I knew he loved me but I still wanted my baby. That was someone who I knew wouldn't leave me and would love me no matter what. Even though I damn near bled to death while going through the miscarriage, I felt like I had to try again. Now I wanted a baby worse than I did at first.

"Derrick" and I proceeded to try again. This time I tried with a vengeance. I was so angry with my mom, I was going to show her that I could do this and I could do it without her. It wasn't long before "Derrick" and I were pregnant again. Actually it was almost six months to the day. This time I waited until I couldn't wait any longer to tell my mom that I was pregnant. I wore big baggie clothes which happened to be the style back then.

It had finally gotten to the point that I was wearing rubber bands around the button of my pants with a big shirt to hide it. When I couldn't hide it anymore, I had come up with a master plan. I was going to get my own place and move out and then tell my mom. I did just that. "Derrick" and I had gotten our own place together and then I waited until one Sunday service right at alter call. I waited until I saw my mom coming down to the alter and then I ran to the back and told her that I was pregnant again and that I was moving out and I took off running out the church doors. I knew that I had to be wise and vigilant for the safety of myself and my baby.

I ran home so fast that even an Olympic champion couldn't catch me. I called "Derrick" as soon as I got home and told him what happened. He assured me he was on his way to come and get me. When he got there, he and I rode back around to the church to see if my mom was there and she was. "Derrick's" mom and my mom were standing outside of the church embracing each other and crying.

For the remainder of my pregnancy I was in between my mom's house, "Derrick's "mom's house and our own place. It was not easy for me to try to have this baby because I was so small and I was so young. I would talk to my baby daily and tell her how much I loved her and how much I needed her and how I was going to protect her at all costs. I promised her that I was going to be the best mom ever and forever it was going to be me, her and her daddy. Then life got real interesting.

Right around seven months I started spotting here and there. The complications began. I was so tired and so was my baby. I knew that I had to make it at all costs. I felt that my baby was about to abandon me as well. Finally the day came when I couldn't stop hurting. My stomach was rock hard and I began bleeding. I had never been so scared in all of my life. I kept talking to my baby and telling her that she had to make it and that my life depended on her.

I was 16 by this time I just knew that I couldn't emotionally handle a miscarriage at 15 and at 16. My mom was finally on board with me and it seemed like everything was lining up I just needed my baby to make it. Then the contractions started. My blood pressure was going up. My stomach was swelling by the minute. I just couldn't believe that all of this was happening to me. No matter what though, I was not there alone. My mom and "Derrick" were there. The doctor was doing all he could to stop the contractions, but they kept coming. Finally my body began to tense up and my limbs began to move and I wasn't moving them. Then I felt as though I couldn't breathe. I was having convulsions. A full blown epileptic seizure is what I was having. Just then, I heard the doctor say that they were going to have to take the baby. I was barely conscious so I couldn't speak to tell them no, as if I had a choice in the matter.

They wind up doing a C-section and taking my baby. She weighed 3 lbs. and 11 ounces. She was 21 inches long. She wasn't breathing on her own nor could she eat on her own. I remember when I was in recovery, they brought the baby for me to see her and I was so heavily sedated, I saw three of them. I was scared to death. My dream had now become a reality. I was a mom!

I had no clue what I was doing and I had no real frame of reference so I was a little lost in the shuffle. My daughter was born at 32 weeks so naturally she had to stay in the hospital for a while until she got her weight up and was able to eat and breathe on her own. I felt like such a failure. This was yet another thing that I messed up.

The two months that she was in the hospital was the longest two months of my life. My mom would tell me to call and check on my baby and I didn't want to because I already felt bad, like a failure. Calling and seeing that she had lost weight or to see that she still wasn't eating or breathing on her own just reminded me how bad I messed up. So I would only really call when my mom made me or when the longing for my baby became too intense. "Derrick" and I would go see her as much as we could as he was working and I was still in school.

Finally after months of prayer, my baby girl was coming home. She was up to four pounds and now she was eating well, and breathing on her own, for the most part. She did have to come home on a monitor for her breathing, but all in all she was ok.

Little did I know this little being would change my life forever.

Life was grand now, so I thought, I had two more people to fill the voids that I had in my life. Little did I know that new voids would be created in a matter of time. "Derrick" and I were doing well. However, he now wanted to go to college. This meant that I now had to work and go to school while taking care of the baby. I was up for the challenge though, as much as I could conceive in my mind.

"Derrick's "mother helped me to get my first job at KFC. My grades were pretty decent still, though my attendance was slacking due to all of the doctor's appointments that the baby and I had. Nevertheless, I made it work. I went to school half day and my mom would watch the baby and then when I went to work "Derrick's "mom would watch her. I didn't really trust anyone else with my baby because she was still too fragile and precious in my eyes.

My brother had come home from Oklahoma for a visit for a season. I found out that he had been in and out of jail a few times but he was also in school. I will never forget the day that he first laid eyes on his niece. He was instantly in love. I think that she made all of us want to be better, even my mom.

My brother had gotten involved with a woman who would help my brother watch my baby from time to time since I was now on my own. Her family wind up falling in love with my baby and they were such a blessing to me. They would take my baby on the weekends so that I could rest or work extra seeing as now I was trying to support "Derrick", my daughter and I on a KFC paycheck, not to mention every time I turned around my mom had her hand out for money from me as well. I was way over extended to say the least. Finally, enough was enough! I was tired of caring for everyone else and I was tired of depending on everyone else so I moved out on my own at the age of 17. I wasn't legal yet to be able to sign my own lease and contracts so I moved in with one of "Derrick's "friends who had agreed to let me and my baby stay.

By this time I was no longer working at KFC I was now at Wal-Mart. Wal-Mart was wonderful about working around my schedule with my daughter and Felix schedule as well because he was helping me with her when everyone else was too busy. I was tired of my mom throwing in my face how she had to help me with my baby so I put a stop to that.

Now my brother had gone away again, "Bob" was out of the picture; "Derrick" was away at college. My mom was acting funny again especially because I refuse to give her money. "Derrick's "mom would help sporadically and Ms. Linda and her family would still take my daughter on the weekends so I could work overtime. I was really maneuvering my way into this motherhood thing. I was finally getting the hang of it. Then the hit of my life came.

I got a call from my mom and she was frantic. I could barely understand what she was saying. She was screaming and crying in the phone. All I could do was grab my baby and run to my mom's rescue. When I got to her house, she was crying like I had never seen before. After talking and coaching her to calm down and talk, I got the news that my Aunt J had been found dead. Aunt J was my mother's baby sister who had some dependency issues. I am still unclear as to what happened but I can say that it rocked my mom to the core. Aunt J was the first of the six girls to die.

My mom went home for the funeral and all. I didn't go because I was on a mission for my baby and me. I couldn't afford to miss any school, nor could I afford to miss any work. Besides, I didn't know much about my aunt anyway. I had only seen her a few times in my whole life.

When that saga was over, mom returned home and we were now at least on speaking terms. In fact, mom had kept trying to get me to come home again, but I refused. I was over the drama and I was doing well for myself and my baby. Now little did I know I was just waiting for the ax to fall yet again.

Felix had to work late one day, and I needed a ride to work. No one was available so I called my mom and she came to take me to work. She had been in contact with me asking me to come home, but I steadily refused. I just didn't want the drama in my life no more. I wanted to protect my baby at all costs. When my mom came and picked me up from my house and took me to work I could tell that she had been crying. I wasn't sure why so I asked.

"I need you to come home Lolo." She cried. "I am going to have to go to the hospital for some tests and this time I am really scared."

I have to admit, I looked at her with a bit of a side eye because I felt that she was just doing it for pity or attention and I wasn't falling for that game anymore. Then she said something that really struck a nerve with me. She looked at me and said, "I would really hate to go to this surgery and then I never see my son again." I was floored! Again, she was longing for the son who seemingly didn't give a damn about us. My brother was home for a minute and then he just up and disappeared again. Yet every time my mother needed something I was always the one she called when none of her many boyfriends couldn't or wouldn't come through. I was done.

I went to work with this on my mind. I couldn't believe that all she still wanted and cared about was her long lost son who was never around anyway. Before I could get all the way fed up, I felt a pulling of the Lord to calm down and think rationally. He had me to replay the occurrences in my mind and to think about the fact that my mother had never cried like that before, nor had she ever pleaded for me to come home like that. When I looked at it from every angle, I was left with no choice but to reassess the situation.

When Felix picked me up that night from work, I told him about what had happened. He too said that I should be there for her, but it did not necessarily mean that I had to move back home to be there. He offered me his car whenever I needed it to go and check on her and to help take care of her. I was at a lost. I felt that there was a crossroad before me and I had no direction which way to go. I had called "Derrick" and I was talking to him about it as well, but he was so involved in college now I didn't feel like he was even giving me his undivided attention.

The day of her surgery had come and her now fiancé' and I took her to the hospital. Ms. Linda kept my baby so that I could be there for my mom. The doctors told us that it would be a few hours for the surgery so he and I decided to go to the mall and grab a bite to eat. We wind up doing some extra shopping and he got a few things for her while I got a few things for my baby.

Neither of us was prepared for what we would return to. We got back to the hospital and we were told to wait in the waiting room still. We waited and waited and waited for what seemed to be an eternity. Finally, a nurse came and said that they had called for us several times with no success. She rushed us to the floor my mom was on. I walked in the room and I was in no way prepared for the vision I saw. My mom was on a ventilator. I had never encountered death or anything close to it before so I had no clue as to what was going on.

From nowhere my mom's best friend, Sheila, came. I knew it was time to cry when I saw her cry because I had never seen that sight from her before. She saw me sitting in the chair next to my mom's bed. I guess she could tell from the look on my face that I had no clue what was going on. That chair was the place that I stayed glued to for days. My cycle was on I didn't care. My baby was with Ms. Linda so I knew that she was fine. I didn't care about work, school, and nothing else. I just knew that I was never going to leave my mom's side again.

I could tell she was trying to say something but I didn't know what since she had the ventilator in her mouth. I could tell she was in pain from the look in her eyes. She would constantly hit the nurse's button to give her something for pain. She and the nurse had this pact that whenever my mom was in pain, she would put her leg over the rail of the bed. The pain had become so intense that my mom just propped her leg over the side of the bed on the rail and left it there. I felt so helpless. I couldn't do anything for her. The whole time she was laying there I kept asking her if there was anything that I could do and she would just look at me. I can only imagine what was going on in her head.

I sat there for two days. I refused to leave. I was afraid to leave, I couldn't think of what would happen if I did. So many memories came flooding to my mind of how I always felt that she was too evil to die. She had to live. Dying was not even an option. I remember she used to tell me and my brother to make sure we didn't cry at her funeral. "Y'all better not shed one damn tear!" she would say. After she would get out of the car, we would look at each other and snicker saying, "I ain't going to cry, are you?" We would then laugh and get out the car. Who would've thought this day was finally approaching.

While I am sitting there watching her suffer, it was like my whole life was flashing before me. I remembered the days that seemed so dark and bleak to me, the days when I was so angry with her. Part of me wanted to scream, the other part wanted to cry, the other part was just numb. This lady gave birth to me. I owed her everything. All of a sudden none of the wrong she done to me mattered. Right when I made that resolve, I looked over at my mom for the first time in a long time and told her that I loved her and I needed her to get better. I looked deep into her eyes and let know that I even forgave her. "Wait, where did that come from? Do I really mean it? How can I do that after all she had done to me? ""It doesn't matter anymore!" "Get over it!" "Grow up!" These words and thoughts were the battles going on in my head and my heart. My intellect said, "Die Bitch, you getting what you deserve after all you done to me!" My heart said, "Honor thy father and mother that your days may be long!" My humanity said, "Go ahead and go, no one deserves to suffer like this!" I wish I could properly articulate the pain that I was in, as well as the turmoil. Right then I saw a tear roll down the side of my mother's face. I now take that tear as her heartfelt apology.

Just then a doctor had come in. This was a doctor that I had never seen before. He made me leave the room and I fought him tooth and nail not to go. He assured me it was only for a moment. I have no idea where this doctor came from, as I stated before I had never seen him before. After a few minutes of him conferring with my mom, whatever that meant, he told me that I could return to the room.

When I walked in my mom was looking at me with this painful stare. I asked him what was wrong with her and why was she looking like that. He told me, "Oh, she's doing better! Tomorrow we are going to be taking her off of the ventilator and trying to get her to breathe on her own." He went on to give me all of these empty assurances that she was coming around and everything was going to be fine. I was little confused but I wanted to believe everything that he was saying. I looked at my mom and she still had this look on her face.

The doctor urged me to go home and shower and get some real rest and take care of my baby. "Baby?? Wait how did he know that I had a baby?" I thought to myself, but he was saying all of these great things, it didn't dawn on me until after I got home. I asked my mom how she felt about it and she just nodded her head for me to go. Little did I know that would be her last request and as usual I obeyed with much hesitation.

I called Sheila, my mom's best friend, and told her what had happened and she told me that she was already on her way. While I waited I sat there and just looked at my mom. Part of me felt that something wasn't right. I now know it was my discernment. There were a few times in between dozes that my mom would look at me and our eyes would make contact. It was as if our hearts were talking to one another without our mouths saying a word. I knew she loved me and vice versa.

Sheila finally arrived and sat a few minutes, even she knew something wasn't right. She went and asked the nurses to see the doctor after I told her what was going on and they told her that the doctor had left for the night. My mom could barely stay awake and didn't seem up for visitors so Sheila and I left. It was a long ride home and neither of us had much to say. All that was in the forefront of my mind was seeing my baby and holding her tight. I was receiving updates from Ms. Linda, Ms. Rita ("Derrick's "mom) and Felix, so I knew she was okay but I just needed to see her.

I finally got back home and Sheila had assured me that I needed to get some sleep. I told her that all I wanted was to see my baby. She said that's fine, but you are not going to be any good to her in your condition. I disagreed with her until I went inside and took a shower and sat there as I waited for them to bring my baby so that I could see her. I went into my own personal coma. It wasn't until Felix came home and unlocked the door that I even knew I was asleep.

He asked me for an update on my mom and I am not even sure that I was able to give him the update before falling back asleep. He was only home for a second when he had to go back to work and I was back to sleep. It seemed like only minutes had passed when I got the call that I had dreaded my whole life. Of course they didn't tell me over the phone, but the doctor called and said that I needed to get back to the hospital immediately. My heart sank. I had no idea what was going on, but I knew it couldn't be good. I immediately called Sheila and told her that I couldn't drive myself to the hospital. She immediately woke up and said, "I am on my way to you!" I sat there and what was literally about ten minutes felt like ten hours.

As soon as I saw her headlights, I took off running out of the door. She skeeted around the curve of the trailer park and we immediately hit the highway to get to my mom which was a good 30-45 minute drive. Sheila ran every red light, surpassed every speed limit. We were both cussing and fussing because she was doing it intentionally in hopes of getting stopped and getting a police escort to the hospital and of course there was none in sight. Sheila lit up a cigarette and she I and I turned into smoky and the bandit. It was the original puff, puff, pass syndrome, only we were only smoking a cigarette. Sadly enough, I wasn't even a smoker.

Finally we get to the hospital. I don't even remember stopping the car before we both took off into the hospital. It was the middle of the night and there a security guard on duty who was expecting us. How? I have no clue! We told him our names and we took off running to her room. Little did we know there were security guards following us. Finally we got to the floor where my mom was and we were almost to the door of her room when the doctors, nurses and security guards stopped us. Sheila saw the closed blinds and immediately started crying ferociously. I had no idea what was going on as I had never experienced anything like this before.

When I saw Sheila crying I knew something had to be wrong. I went bananas. I just wanted to see my mom. I had to see her! I had to let her know that I was there. I tried and tried to get to her room but the security guard just picked me up and took me into the conference room. I fought him the whole way. When we got into the conference room the doctor came in and I looked to the right and saw Sheila shivering as though she was sitting in the arctic cold. She kept looking at me and crying and saying my name over and over, "Lolo?? Lolo??" I had no idea why she was doing that. There were two big security guards there on my left and Sheila was on my far right with the doctor sitting between us. He looked at me and said, "We called you at 2:19am and she died at 2:32am. I went berserk. I tore that whole waiting room up. I don't know who was doing what or who was where; all I know is that I was pissed.

"I told you all, I didn't want to leave but you insisted!" I screamed. "Where is that damn flaky ass doctor that told me she was getting better?" I asked. The doctor looked at me and said, "I am her only doctor!"

I told him, "No you're not, there was another one!" I described the other doctor to the tee and the doctor assured me that there was no doctor that fit that description. I proceeded to tell him that he was crazy and all I wanted at this point was to see my mama. I was not going to believe it until I seen it myself.

"We will not let you back there until you calm down, Lolo"

"Calm down? Calm down? What the hell does that mean? Let me kill your mama and see how calm you are," I said. "I want to see my mama and I want to see her NOW!!"

"Calm down first!" The doctor ordered.

Sheila came over there and grabbed me and held me tight and said, "Lolo, she never liked to see you like this."

I looked at Sheila and everything within me calmed down for the moment. The nurse came and gave me and Sheila some medicine. I wouldn't take it until Sheila took hers. I soon begin to feel calmer on the inside and by this time mom's fiancé' had arrived. He took one look at the waiting room and immediately knew what had happened. He grabbed me and held me tight as any father should, though I didn't know him like that. He and Sheila took me by the hand and walked me into the room where my mom was.

My feet felt like bricks. Those 50 feet felt like 50 miles. The hospital is already cold but now it felt like an artic breeze that stood still over my body. We walked in the door and all of the tubes were gone. She was laying there covered as though she was just sleeping. The leg that I was used to seeing hanging over the rails was now in its normal resting position. The lady I saw on that bed was the lady that I knew. That was my mama.

There are five stages of grief and I believe I went through them all that night. I was in denial thinking what is going on here to no, this cannot be happening. Then I went through the angry stage where I tore the whole damn waiting room up. Thirdly, when we entered into the room I immediately went into the bargaining stage saying, "God, if you bring her back, I promise, I will move back home. If you bring her back I will forgive her for everything she done and I won't bring it up again. God, just bring her back please!!" From that bargaining, stage I went back to the anger phase mad at her for leaving me before I could prove her wrong when she kept declaring that I would never be anything. She said I would never finish high school and I was months away from graduating. I had to show her that I could and would be better than she had ever hoped for my life but she died before I could. I had no way of knowing that this pursuit of proving her wrong would become a lifelong pursuit. I had no way of knowing that years later I would still be trying to prove her wrong. Sad but true.

When we left my mom's room and everyone said their goodbyes, we went to the pay phone and called my aunts and my grandmother. Mind you they had just buried my aunt J six months earlier. I don't think anyone was ready for this. I remember talking to Aunt B and she assured me that they were still coming and everything was going to be alright. I didn't know if I was going or coming. I called Felix and told him. He told me that he would be home waiting for me. I called Linda and told her and she told me not to worry about my daughter that she had her and she would be well taken care of and that they would be there to help me. Finally, I called "Derrick's" mom and she got in touch with him and told him what was going on. This was the longest night of my life.

I had never experienced death before, only what I had seen on television and there, the people die and then there was a funeral. I never knew what happened from one phase to the other. Sheila and the hospital had to explain to me the process. Okay now, there is only so much that this 18 year old can endure in one night. They instructed me to go home and rest and start making decisions tomorrow. For once I listened.

I went home and demanded my baby come home and lay with me. They brought her to me in the middle of the night and all I could do was cry and hold her. "Derrick" called and told me he was on his way home in the morning. I didn't know how I felt. My everything was still numb and I was still walking around in disbelief.

I got up the next day and went to my school and talked to my principal. I later found out she already knew everything that was going on with me via my teachers and friends who had taken it upon themselves to raise some money for me. I then went to my job at Wal-Mart and told them what was happening. My boss asked me if I had any siblings. I had forgotten all about my brother in the midst of it all. I told her yes, I have a brother but I don't know where he is. She asked me where was the last place that I knew him to be and I told her Oklahoma. She immediately asked me for his full name and any other identifying information that I had which was his name, birthdate and a picture. She immediately went to work and posted the picture of him in all of the Wal-Mart's in the area near which he reportedly lived.

Two days before the funeral, we got a call from my brother. My aunts, Uncle R and my grandmother were in town now and they were helping me tremendously to certain degree. This was when I went through my depression stage of the grieving process. My family, as all families do, kept saying that they wanted this and wanted that and I personally didn't care because none of it was going to bring her back. I then went to the leasing office of my mom's apartment and they informed me that I had seven days from the day she died to move all of her belongings out of the apartment because I was not on the lease, I could not stay in her apartment, not that I wanted to anyway. Now I was in a pickle.

I was living in a mobile home with Felix; my mother had a three bedroom apartment with European furniture in it that would easily put a hole in the floor if I brought it to his place. All I could do was pray and wait. Just then I got a call from the leasing office saying that they had found me an apartment in another apartment complex and I qualified to move over there. Thank you Jesus! I was inside the house and was talking to the family about it all when there was a knock on the door. It was the police! What NOW??? I asked myself. They asked for Sheila. First thing that I thought of was that they had pictures of her speeding that night. I had no clue and my mind couldn't think of anything else.

Just then Sheila busted back in the door crying again. I was lost! Finally she told us that her husband had just had a massive heart attack and was rushed to the hospital. We all hollered, "Oh Lord NO!!!" We all rushed to go be with Sheila. When we got to the hospital, I realized I couldn't do it. He was in the same hospital my mom had just died in. He was on the same floor and even worst they had the same doctor. He was only two doors down from where my mom had died. It was too much!

Sheila told them to get me out of there and they agreed it was too much for me. They gave me more meds and took me home. By the time I got home, he had died. This was a whole other level of "more than I could bear!" When we got home and were just processing that news the phone rang. It was my brother. He had talked to the family, as in my aunts and grandmother and then he asked to speak to me. I took the phone and the first words out of his mouth were, "How could you let this happen, Lolo?" I was flabbergasted. I didn't have a response for him. As a matter of fact I just simply gave the phone back to my grandmother because I had been through enough. I did give him time to let me know that he would be home in time enough for the funeral. Little did I know the family had planned another funeral for Texas so that all of the children (nieces and nephews) could attend. I thought long and hard about it. I just couldn't do two funerals. I was there through her suffering, I was there through her pain, I had walked through all of the arrangements and I still had to sit through a funeral. All at the age of 18 with a baby that was just a little over a year old, not to mention that I was still trying to finish school and I had to move and get back to work so that I could take care of my baby and I.

I was thinking of all of this when we had to go to the funeral home and preview my mom's body after she was dressed. I thought it be best that I take my baby with me so that she could say goodbye to her grandmother. When we got there, My daughter saw my mother laying there looking like she was asleep and My daughter tried to jump out of my arms to get to my mom to take her glasses off which was something that she always done. That was when I lost it. It had all overtaken me and I felt like I couldn't go another further.

I finally broke the news to my family that I would not be attending the second funeral in Texas. I told them that I could barely do the funeral here, Georgia. They were very disappointed to say the least. I went on to ask them if they were all going to come back and help me move all of her stuff since they knew that I was on a time constraint. I had seven days from the day she died to move. She died on a Saturday, I found out about it that Monday, her funeral in Georgia was on Wednesday and the Texas funeral was Friday. I had to pack and then I had to move, and not to mention find people to help me move. I made up my mind and I stuck with my decision.

Doomsday had arrived. It was the day of my mother's Georgia funeral. I was still not ready, but there was nothing that I could do about it now. I had cried all that I could cry; I bounced around between grief, acceptance and depression. I was drained and exhausted in every way possible. My brother had made it that morning. "Derrick" had made it as well. Sheila had decided to have her husband's funeral the same day but his was at the funeral home while my mom's was at the church. We had notified "Bob" and he chose to go to Sheila's husband's funeral over my mom's. For the life of me at that time I couldn't understand his logic but in the moment I didn't care either. I just wanted to get through my mother's funeral in one piece.

I chose to ride to the funeral alone, just "Derrick" and I because I had been around and through enough with my family, I just wanted some peace. My feelings and emotions were everywhere. I didn't even know how I felt about "Derrick" anymore. Him being gone to college drew a bit of a wedge between us but I did not know how to explain or accept that.

We finally arrived at the church and it was packed. There were cars for miles. I suddenly knew that I wasn't as ready as I thought that I was. We got there and my body froze. I couldn't even get out of the car for a minute. "Derrick" gave me a pep talk as did everyone else but still inside I felt as though no one knew what I was really going through and though my vocabulary was large, I knew no words to express the way I felt. Numb was too shallow, empty was too grave, bitter and broken seemed too temporary so I just shut down and said nothing.

My brother came and helped me out of the car. We walked to the church together. Hand in hand just like the old days only there was no more real connection like before. As we entered the church, all eyes were on us. I was the most uncomfortable because I was already nervous that I wouldn't and couldn't make it. We kept walking. My knees tried to buckle. The tears felt like a tsunami coming from my face. My heart felt as though it shattered more with every step that I took.

Finally, we made it to her coffin. Oh the emotions that I felt. I remember part of me thinking, "I still can't believe this!" Another part of me looked at her face and said, "You can't hurt me anymore!" One part of me even wanted to slap her dead face in anger because she died before I could prove her wrong about me never being nothing and never finishing high school. I remember as a kid my mom would always tell us that her prayer was Lord, you can take me anytime you want to, I just want to see my kids get grown and graduate high school and then I can consider my work done.

Her dying before I was able to graduate high school felt like another slap in the face, another slight that I got from her. She was there for my brother's prom and graduation. She even was the driver for him and his girlfriend for prom. I was on my own and left to my own devices. I was so angry.

My brother and friends finally pulled me away from the coffin and interrupted my combustible thoughts that had erupted in my mind. I don't remember much of what happened at the funeral as I was in a zone of survival. I just wanted it to be over as soon as possible and I felt an earthquake within with a Richter scale through the roof coming up within me.

Please don't sing another song, don't say another word, just give the benediction so we can go. I do remember looking over to my left and seeing some of my mom's friends from Germany as well as a host of other people that we had not seen in forever. Come on people, this is too much! Can it be over already? No? Okay. I remember the choir getting up to sing yet another song and I crumbled. The tears tried to make me swim out of the church! The anger pushed me over the edge of sanity! My feet went into overdrive and I took off out of the church. I told them I couldn't take anymore but they wanted to keep going. Everybody got to say something. This one wants to sing, this one wants to preach, this one wants to testify. Just too much so I bailed and I kept hollering, "I can't do this, I just can't do this!" People came running out of the church doors and tried to console me. Little did they know that my only consolation at that moment was, "Leave me the hell alone and get out my face!"

Finally they all got the hint. "Derrick" took me back home and I don't remember anything else from that funeral. I just went home and started packing up all her stuff to prepare to move in a few days. My family was still barely speaking to me because I refused to go to the funeral in Texas. "That's fine. They are leaving tomorrow anyway!" I said to myself.

The next day came and my family loaded up and left to go to Texas for the Friday funeral. Now it was time for my new journey to begin, whatever that looked like. Whatever it was, it had to be better than this. Mom's death felt like rock bottom and there was nowhere to go but up from there.

Divine Revelation

In this chapter I realized my errors of trying to fill the voids of my losses of "Bob" and my brother with "Derrick" and my daughter. I realize that this action was unfair, not only to "Derrick", but especially to my daughter. She came into this world with an expectation and though she has lived up to that expectation of loving me unconditionally, it still wasn't a fair demand to put on her. I feel that the void that I filled with them was only magnified at the loss of my mom. That is a void that can and will never be filled

12

AGAINST MY WILL BUT WE MADE IT!-BIRTH OF MY SON

Chapter Foreword by my son

My mother is a strong and magnificent mom. She is very independent, faithful and always a motivator and no one knows that better than me. Every time I see, hear or think of Lolo, mom as I call her, I think that she is always going to bring something positive in to the lives of others just like she did for me.

Life for me was tough with the disability and trying to learn how to function normally, or even with help for that matter. I wasn't aware that I was planned, but not wanted to some degree so I never focused on it and I really couldn't tell because all of my life I knew that no matter what, my mom loved me. Even though our relationship has had its ups and downs, her love for me has remained consistent.

Though she had her shortcomings by showing what she called "tough love" like the time I was caught messing around in the house while she was away so she took my key and told me I had to sit outside and wait until she or my sister came home every day. Even the time that she and I went toe to toe in the front yard because I thought I was the man and could go and come as I please under her roof. (My mom is much stronger than she looks; don't let the small package fool you). Even through the times that I felt she showed favoritism towards my sister, I knew three things for sure. My mom loves me, supports me and she pushes me which is why I am the man that I am today!

The Journey Continues...

--------◆◆◆◆◆--------

Well the immediate storm of my mom's death has now passed and now it is time to pick up the pieces and move on with my life, whatever that looked like. First order of business was to get out of high school and also get back to work. I was now living on my own in a whole new apartment, it was fully furnished, mostly with my mom's stuff and everything was paid for including my car. I think I got a pretty good head start on the remainder of my life. "Derrick" had quit college to come home and help me with my daughter.

For once it seemed as though my dreams were coming together or at least I thought. Mom died in February, by March I was pregnant again with another baby. This time I knew I didn't want any more kids. After all, I had died trying to have the one that I got. "Derrick", however, wanted a boy, as if it were a guarantee that it would be so. Did I have a choice other than to meet the needs of my man? I didn't think so, so we did it. We got pregnant in March and got married in April. Now here I am last year of high school. A mother of one, pregnant with another, married, working, grieving, confused and clueless. All I knew for sure is that I had to graduate because even though my mom was gone, I still had to prove her wrong, I would graduate high school.

Even though I was a senior, I had missed a lot of days from doctor's appointments for My daughter, the death of my mom, and just life in general I couldn't miss any more days for fear of not graduating so even though I was already having issues with this pregnancy, I refused to miss school, even when the doctor put me on bed rest.

This was my most difficult pregnancy from start to finish. The biggest issue is that I didn't want to be pregnant in the first place. Secondly, I felt clueless to life and where I was going beyond high school and all I knew

70

currently was the diploma was my only goal at this point. I knew that I was pregnant almost immediately. What I didn't know immediately is that I was pregnant with twins. TWO??? Are you serious? Yes, I was pregnant with twin boys, "Derrick" was ecstatic and I was livid.

I was stressed beyond measure with my life and it costs. I was always about my regular routine. Get up, take my daughter to her babysitter, go to school, leave there and go to work. "Derrick" would pick her up when he got off. After work I would come home and study and do my homework as well as cook, clean, get My daughter prepared for the next day and oh yeah by the way, trying to be super wife by trying to sex him up daily to keep him happy, so I thought. It was all too stressful and it caused me to start having pains. These were not just normal pains but feeling nearly like labor pains. With each one, I knew more and more that I was not down for this new baby stuff.

I still wanted to keep my life as normal as I could, after all, it was my senior year and I wanted to enjoy this last year. I went to prom, with a belly; I went on the senior trip to Disney world, with a belly. I did everything during my senior year with a belly and I was not happy about it. Little did I know that resentment would only grow as the babies within me grew.

Finally the big day had arrived! It was graduation time! I had my cap, my gown, my pictures, my baby girl, my man…all in tow. Then it hit me, I have no family! Mom was gone, everyone had just left for the funeral so I knew they wouldn't come back to support me because they were all still upset that I didn't go the Texas funeral they had for my mom. Then my cousin Felicia and Ava surprised me and came to my graduation as did "Bob", Sheila and my mom's fiancé Mr. Ned. This was all great but I was still unhappy and now back in my feeling because again I felt shortchanged that my mom had the audacity to die on me before seeing me graduate and then on top of that my brother didn't show up either. How could he? Doesn't he remember that we are all we have right now? How could he betray me this way? Just then in the middle of my emotional madness, this pain came from nowhere. It was pretty bad, but I knew that there was no way I was going to miss my graduation.

I was at the beginning because my last name was still my maiden name on my records so I was able to make it to get my diploma and then just sit there and rock back and forth through this whole experience. Again I am forced to sit through something that was the most uncomfortable for me, but I couldn't just walk out after getting my diploma, so I sat and I sat for hours until they were done. Finally, it was over and I stood up to throw my cap and guess what? I was sitting in a puddle of stuff. I had on all black so I was not sure what it was but I was not going to ruin my day that I had waited on for so long just to see what it was.

Even through the hurt and the pain and the leaking, I still enjoyed my graduation night. My cousins left the next day and went back to Texas, "Derrick" had to work, my daughter was gone with her God parents and I was home alone laying there in secret pain that I told no one about. Finally, I couldn't take it no more and I went to the doctor. The news that I received was the most devastating. I had miscarried one of the boys. I had no idea what that meant. The doctor finally explained to me that because they didn't share the same sack that I could continue on with the pregnancy under strict and close supervision and I had to be on bed rest.

They said that if it were earlier in my pregnancy, it would not be as risky because it would be the normal vanishing twin syndrome, which is where the baby's tissue would be absorbed by the other twin, the placenta or the mother, but mine was a bit more severe because it caused me to have seizures and other side effects.

As I went through this "Derrick" was working and My daughter was enjoying her little life with her fan club called her grand and God parents and I was again left at home alone to suffer through this trauma. Not knowing if I was ever going to give birth. Would there be something wrong with the baby? What if I have another premature birth? Who will be there this time since mom was gone. Again I am left to sit there and think about all of the things that could go wrong and the more I thought, the more I suffered.

The cramps, the spotting, the bleeding, the sickness, after a while I began to think that God was punishing me about lying about my desire to have another baby. I had to put off college, could not enjoy life with my own baby because I am lying in bed suffering. This feeling of abandonment made me start to resent "Derrick" and this baby inside of me that I really didn't want in the first place. This drew a wedge between us and we began to have an on again off again relationship even though we were married.

Time went on and my pregnancy began to normalize into the normal

Vanishing Twin Syndrome, but my pregnancy was still considered high risk so I was there at the doctor nearly every week, no more than every two weeks again alone as usual. This went on for months. They couldn't understand the growth of my stomach nor my son. One side of my stomach grew but the other one didn't. I was so embarrassed that I didn't ever really want to go outside; I didn't want to be seen. "Derrick" began to lose his attraction to me and would sometimes make fun of me and my size. He would call me all sorts of names, but I tried to keep on loving him anyway. After all, I was used to being called names. After what seemed like forever, my growth began to normalize a bit and my stomach began to even out. I was good for about a month, no sickness, no bleeding, no cramps and finally no period. We thought we were out of the woods and then…

I went back to work trying to normalize my life again. I was a cashier at Wal-Mart which meant that I was always on my feet which was against doctor's orders, but I had to do something because my life seemed so out of control. At this point, I didn't care whether the baby made it or not. I felt like my life was in complete disarray because of it. I missed lots of moments with my baby; I didn't even enjoy my first summer out of high school. I wasn't able to enjoy my senior year, my graduation, nothing. I felt as though I had made the ultimate sacrifice for a man who didn't give a damn because he was in and out of our relationship and he was free to move around but I wasn't because I was left holding the baggage that he wanted even though I didn't.

Now keep in mind, I got pregnant with my daughter in March and she was due in December and so it was with my son as well. My daughter was born in October so the doctor had already said that due to the complications of my first pregnancy that when October came that I would be coming to see him at least twice every week to make sure that everything remained normal especially given all that we had already been through. Well guess what? They were both born in October. October 19, one week before my daughter's second birthday, I gave birth to my son. Same scenario, different child. His was more severe so I don't remember much of it. I know that I was having really bad seizures; they could not stabilize my blood pressure. I believe at one point they came and told "Derrick" that it was either me or the baby. I didn't even want to know what his decision was but nevertheless we both lived.

My son was born October 19, 1993 as a single baby. He was smaller than my daughter; he only weighed 2 pounds and 14 ounces. He was really touch and go for a season.

After I gave birth, I had more issues than a little bit. I miss my daughter's second birthday party because I was in the hospital still recovering from giving birth. I often found myself alone in the hospital room. I couldn't really see the baby because he was taken to another hospital and placed in the neonatal unit. "Derrick" was working, mom was gone, my family was all in Texas and I was still in Georgia, my daughter was too small to come and see me, so again I was all alone left to deal with this issue. Then the worst happened…

They released me from the hospital almost two weeks later. I had an infection in my incision from my C-section so they ripped it back open and sent me home with an open stomach and a home health nurse who would come over 3 times a day to clean my womb. Naturally, I couldn't go back to work for a while, I couldn't enjoy my oldest child. My marriage was a wreck and my life seemed the same. Then of all things they have a major shoot out in my apartment complex. Now on top of all of this I have to move because I was fearful for me and my daughter's safety.

On top of all of that the bad news just kept coming. My son's doctor calls and tells me that I need to come in and see him ASAP. What? What could this mean? Did they find something? Did he die? The last time a doctor called and talked to me like that it was because my mom had passed. I rushed to the hospital, need I say alone? I get there and the nurse places me in the office of the doctor, there were no blinds and security guards so I assumed we were safe that my baby was still alive at least but what was this call for and why did I have to drive one hour away to sit in an office all by myself looking around at a library and a desk, left to think of all of these things that I could be, little did I know my life was about to change forever.

The doctor finally comes in after what seemed like an eternity. He greets me and I was so in my feelings, I remember thinking, "Get to the point man, why am I here?" He turns on this light and shows me these images, as if my 18 year old self knew what I was looking at. He sits down and tells me, "I have good news and I have bad news, which would you like first?"

"Look man, ain't nobody got time for this win, lose or draw stuff, just give it to me straight no games." I said.

He looks at me and echoes words that would change my very existence, "You baby has a birth defect."

"What? What the hell does that mean? What? Come on? Not now, not later, not ever! Are you sure?" I cried.

He goes on to explain, "Your baby has Agenesis of the Corpus Callosum which is a rare birth defect (congenital disorder) in which there is a complete or partial absence of the corpus callosum, the band of white matter connecting the two hemispheres in the brain, fails to develop normally, typically during pregnancy"

"What? What the hell does that mean? What? Come on? Not now, not later, not ever! Are you sure?" I cried again.

"Yes, we ran the test several times, here is a picture of a regular brain, here is the picture of a brain with is condition," he said.

"So what does this mean though," I asked?

He went on to tell me all of these things that my child may never do. Nothing heavy just, he will never walk, talk, hear, or see. Just four of the five senses. I froze in my chair. I looked up and thought to myself, "—for real God? You hate me too? Why do I have to go through this and why do I have to do this alone? If you were going to make my life miserable like this why even bring me to this earth? I was so angry and that anger haunts me sometimes even to this very day.

I got in my car and went to the hospital to see my son. I talked to the nurses and they told me he was doing better and may be going home soon. I didn't know how I felt about that before, but especially now. From the day I got the news of his condition, I never looked at my son the same. I saw him as a fragile little flower and there was nothing fragile or gentle about me that I could handle him in that manner.

The comparisons started almost immediately. I compared him to my daughter. She was 3 pounds and 11 ounces and he was only 2 pounds and 14 ounces. My pregnancy with her was nearly textbook perfect, yet with him I missed out on life and all of the festivities that I was supposed to enjoy during my senior year of high school. I had weekends off with my daughter because she was gone almost every weekend with her grandparents or her God parents who helped me in every way with her but made it abundantly clear that they were not going to help me with the second child because they didn't agree with the decisions that I was making. Little did they know I was not making them alone. Hell, I didn't agree with some of the decisions that I "appeared" to be making.

I was so resentful of him that I never looked at the fact that my son gained weight faster than My daughter, he got to go home quicker than My daughter, he breathed on his own before My daughter did and most importantly he didn't have to come home with a breathing machine like she did. All I could focus on with him was the negative, because of the inner feelings and thoughts that I felt and now to find out he was less than perfect was more than I could bear.

I rushed home and told "Derrick" about what happened and what the doctor said. He looked at me as though he had seen a ghost. He began asking me questions that I couldn't answer. Unfortunately, this was all before the internet so it wasn't like we could go and Google his condition and how to deal with it so I was heavily dependent upon the resources that the doctor gave me.

There was so much responsibility to my son that I didn't know if I could handle it all. He had physical therapy, occupational therapy, eventually there was speech therapy, but for me there was no therapy. I was clueless as to what to do and what to expect so one day in conversation I began to tell one of his therapists how I felt and she connected me with and agency that practiced linking families together with other families whose children had the same diagnoses. My son's defect was so rare that it was hard to find a match in the database that was close to me but by me living in a military town, there was a family that moved there and they set it up for me to go and meet this child who was then 15 years old.

I was excited to meet him and his family. I had so many questions. They didn't give me much information about the kid, everything that I asked they just said, "Wait until you meet the family and you will see for yourself and ask them all the questions in the world." I thought they were just leaving me in suspense, I didn't realize that under the law they couldn't tell me anything.

The day finally came and I went to the home of these people and that was a life altering experience for me. I walked into the door of their home and met his mom and his step dad. He had other siblings, one of which was outside playing basketball; all along I thought he was the kid that I was coming to see. Little did I know that the person that I was coming to see was sitting in the den. They walked me to see him. When I go to the door my knees nearly buckled. I saw this huge boy sitting in this contraption that propped him up. This baby at 15 could not walk, talk, see, sit up, he was still in diapers, and they even still had to feed him through a tube. OH MY GOODNESS!!! Was all I could think! I did all I could to hold it together and not cry while I was in the presence of these people. After all, the first thing that the mom told me was how strong I appeared to be. The family was so gracious that they allowed me to ask them anything and they answered openly and honestly.

When I finally walked out of the house, I raced to my car and sped off. I went to the park and sat there and cried and screamed and screamed and cried. I talked to God in laymen's terms. I told him exactly how I felt, I didn't follow a model prayer, I created one just for me. It went just like this;

"Look here man,

I don't know what the problem is between us, but you promised not to put more on me than I can bear, but right now you are taking me to the limits, beyond my limits if I be honest. Just this year alone, you have taken my mom, let me marry a man who doesn't love me, taken the fun out of my senior year experience. I have lain around for months and did nearly everything that the doctor told me to do so can you PLEASE give me a break? I don't know how to do all of this and I don't know what is in store for me but that, that I just left, I CANNOT handle so please show me how to get through this and let's make it happen because I just can't."

I remember this prayer like it was yesterday, and from that moment on the fight bad begun. I went and I picked up both of my children and took them home. I prayed over them as though it was my last time. I lifted them up like the man in roots and I literally gave them and myself back to God.

"Derrick" came home from work and broke the news to me that he was going to go into the army. Just then I was again enraged but I remembered the prayer that I had just prayed. That's when I knew that I was in the fight of my life for me and my children's sake. We had a few months before he was to leave so Christmas had come and I knew this was 's first Christmas and I wanted to really make this Christmas special for my daughter especially since I missed her second birthday party. Then my son gets sick and winds up in the hospital. He was now in a regular hospital with no real nursery for him so he had to have a parent with him at all times. I was stuck and couldn't really leave because only God knew where "Derrick" was, again my daughter was with her Godparents again and I was stuck there with my son. My church members came by to visit, but little did they know how angry I was.

"Derrick" left a bitter taste in my mouth when he left, even though it seemed to be a noble act to go fight for his country, but I would rather him fight for his family and not leave me alone to figure it all out by myself but this abandonment was becoming a commonplace so I sat in it and created my own support system. I got closer into the church. I was doing a little bit of everything but coming home was a constant reminder that I was still in this alone.

It wasn't long before "Derrick" was back home, and I knew that it was over but I wanted to keep my childhood vow. (Remember: 2 children, same father, married, and together forever.) I wanted badly to make it work. We started going to church together and we were radical with it. We got rid of all R&B music, we only listened to Gospel. We lived in the church, too bad the church didn't live in us. We were constantly at each other's throats. He would call me fat, and I would call him a wimp. He would attach my mothering skills, and I would attack his "manhood." It was ugly.

Finally, while in the church, there was a young man in the church who paid me some attention and told me that I was still pretty and that I was an awesome mom and how he had admired my strength. I hadn't heard those words in forever. Needless to say, one thing led to another and I committed adultery. Not making excuses, but "Derrick" was in and out all the time. He was either working, hanging out with his dad or his friends and I was left there to tend to the children ALONE and I was tired of it.

I finally just told "Derrick" about the affair in hopes that it would make him be a better husband to me; we were a year into our marriage but had been together over four years. What was his response? Well, ok that's fine I am going to drive trucks. I have to go to school first, and then they guarantee me a job, but I promise I am going local so I can be home every night. I fell for it!

"Derrick" left to drive trucks, I got back into the church since the guy I had the affair with had left, my son was making progress, my daughter was doing great. It seemed like things were working themselves out. Not! My son was starting to have difficulties again in therapy. It wasn't the first time that they would do something that he couldn't grasp and that was my cue to crank up the prayer. He had already surpassed the kid that I had seen; my son was at least sitting up by himself. He would do little things with his hands to show off his fine motor skills, but his large motor skills were something different. We were coming up on a year and he still couldn't walk and potty training wasn't even on the radar as of yet.

Time had now passed; the men in the church had really stepped up to help me with my son. "Derrick" was home for a visit before his first OVER THE ROAD job assignment. My son barely knew who he was, so naturally there was no trust. "Derrick" would throw him in the air and my son would holler and scream bloody murder. One day, we went to church and one of the guys at the church threw him up in the air and my son just laughed and giggled as he always does. When we got home I heard it.

"What, are you fucking him too?" "Derrick" asked.

I knew then that even though I was being good now, he had not forgiven me. I knew then that it was going to be a long road. I just stayed focused on my kids and hoped that God would work the rest out. Now "Derrick's "parents had a problem with my daughter's God parents and vice versa. "Derrick" had a problem with everyone and I was at peace with everyone because in one way or another they were all helping me out at times. My daughter's God parents were still getting her on the weekends, the grandparents were getting my son on the weekends, sometimes, the church was my safety net and "Derrick" was the father to both of my children and finally I was being good.

Divine Revelation

Sometimes there are occurrences in our life that change our lives. This chapter was a lesson about living in your authentic truths and making personal sacrifices for the one that you love. As much as it hurts me to say it now, I did not want my son. I was torn on how I was supposed to feel. I was grieving my mother, then the loss of one of the twins, then the loss of the completion of my son and eventually beginning to lose my marriage. Originally I felt that it was because I was authentic in my truth of not wanting to have another baby at that time. Then I went on and thought that I was being punished for the disobedience I showed my mother. She always said, "I can't wait for you to have kids so that they can give you back the hell that you gave me and then some." In this season, I believed that I was being punished in a great way.

13

RISE UP-LEFT "DERRICK"

Chapter Foreword by My daughter

With me being so young at the time of this event I only remember bits and pieces of my parents splitting. I remember a few of the arguments and them making up, but there are 2 arguments I remember very well.

One argument is why I thought for so long my parents splitting was my fault. It's when we were at my Grandmother's house and we were next door with the white people playing and I remember my dad and the daughter of the neighbor being friendly which they always were. This day it was different, I can't explain how, it just was. Then my mom pulled up and things went wrong from there. My mom and dad were arguing again but I was asked if my dad was with the girl that day and I answered honestly like always, but the reaction from my honesty changed everything. From that day until the day we left everything was sad, ugly, different, and slow.

The second argument that stays with me to this day is the day I made the first, biggest, most important decision of my life at the age of 4. I had my life in my hands. I was asked who I wanted to spend the rest of my life with my mother or my father. Big decision for such a young age, I wouldn't change a thing but you can't help but to wonder. However, I know now God knew what he was doing.

The Journey Continues…

─────────◆◆◆◆◆─────────

When I realized enough was enough, I had called my Aunt A and told her that I wanted to come home. By this time now My Aunt J had passed, six months later my mom passed and five years later my grandmother had passed. My brother and I came home for the funeral of my grandmother and it felt great being amongst my family again which is what gave me the idea of moving to Texas. Clearly things were not working out between "Derrick" and me. We had split up yet again and this time he was seeing other people and I was considering it but honestly was too tied up with all of my son's needs.

I remember the day that I decided to leave like it was yesterday. I was in the kitchen and the kids were outside with "Derrick". My daughter had just gotten a bike and "Derrick" was out there with her helping her ride. All of a sudden I heard my son hollering and screaming. I ran outside in fear of the worst, after all he was my fragile child. When I get out there I heard "Derrick" saying, "Boy get up, quit acting like a pussy! You can ride this bike! Stop crying!" I had never witnessed him talking to the kids this way, he was normally only abusive to me telling me how fat and ugly I was, but now it had leaked over onto the kids and I knew I wasn't about to stand for that. Mistreat me all you want, I am grown but to be like that towards my kids is a different beast and now I must make some hard decisions. He was living between his girlfriend's house and his parent's house and I was in a mobile home with my kids. All I had was my car note of $301.24 and I was getting no financial support from him. I took that last bit of money, loaded up my kids, their clothes, and their toys in the car and to Texas we went.

I remember feeling like I was running from my life for some reason but there was no need. It's not like "Derrick" wanted the kids or anything, I guess it was just the fact that I had made a decision to break free and would not, nor could not turn back.

My son was doing ok. He had not too long ago learned how to walk. He was just now really learning how to talk, he was potty trained and we were well on our way. God is amazing. The current battle was trying to find a school that I could trust with my baby and whether or not to put a helmet on him for safety reason. My vote was no because I wanted him to lead as normal of a life as possible. We had done so well thus far.

His sister was in school and doing very well, she was ahead of her class and later tagged as gifted and talented. I just believed by faith that my son was going to get some of that because he sat in his high chair everyday as I worked with his sister. We had even created a family sign language for my son to communicate with us what it is he wanted. We taught it to everyone and they all had their own version as well but all that mattered is that we had him communicating until he could learn to talk. Doctors were still baffled at how well he was doing. He had beaten a lot of the odds by this time and he was only three.

Divine Revelation

Just because we leave a situation doesn't mean that we have closure. Closure does not come until there is a release that happens. I left the situation with my kids' father, and I even changed my destination, but I failed to receive that closure that was needed to move on. On one hand I was making progress with my child but emotionally and mentally I was a wreck, not to mention indecisive as to the fate of my relationship. Nevertheless I moved on but that absence of closure cost me greatly later.

14

STEP UP-NEW LIFE IN TEXAS

Chapter Foreword by My best ex-husband

I met Lolo a long time ago, back in the 90's and she has always been the intelligent, beautiful, and smart lady that she is today. If I know nothing else about Lolo, I learned over all of these years that she is going to achieve any and everything that she puts her mind to.

One of the things that attracted me to Lolo is the fact that she is a strong woman, and always comes through things better than when she went in. If I know nothing else about her, I know that she is a child of God.

When I met her, I needed a friend but I stepped out on faith and fell in love. I loved the way that she carried herself, and how well she took care of her kids against all odds. I stepped in the way that I did to assist because it felt like the right thing to do as a man.

I fell in love with the kids because they were caring, loving and respectful to me. Honestly, they also filled in the voids for the children I never had but always wanted.

I am proud of Lolo because she turned out a whole lot greater than I could have ever imagined and her maturity still leaves me speechless. Though she is my ex-wife, I still love and respect her as the mother of my children and my closest friend.

The Journey Continues...

I remember as I was making the drive to Texas I would stop at every state line and say a prayer and shed a few tears because I was forced to reflect on the pain that the life I was living had brought me. I was trying to keep my promise that I made to myself as a kid and was only hurting myself in the meantime.

It had gotten so bad that the kid's grandparents didn't even want me to come around and they would only watch the kids sporadically so I used them as a last resort. I realized that I was breaking free from the bad marriage with "Derrick", the bad relationship with his family, but most of all the bad relationship that I had with myself.

When I finally arrived to Texas I was exhausted. Aunt A was so excited. She had already agreed that we could stay with her. I had not lived with anyone in years; remember I had been on my own since I was sixteen. This was going to take some adjusting. I walked in with goals for myself. This was a complete faith walk as I had no job lined up and I had no idea what I was doing, I just knew that I had to protect me and my kids from all toxic relationships, even if it was their father.

After getting some rest, I sat down with Aunt A and told her what my plan was. I told her to give me 30 days, and I will have a job. Give me 90 days, and we will be out of your house and I will be on my own again. She kept telling me not to rush, but even then I had the belief that every queen needs her own castle. I was on a mission and I meant business. I knew that "Derrick" was not going to help me; after all I didn't even tell him where we were until later.

God was so amazing; he had exceeded even my expectations. Within one week, I had both of my kids in school. I had a job at the local grocery store. I had signed up for all benefits that I could qualify for, and in 30 days

I had my own place again. I wish I could say that it was smooth sailing, but the ride had not even begun yet.

"Derrick" had found us somehow and had contacted my aunt just to ask how we were doing. She assured them that we were fine and told him of how God had blessed me and the kids. He asked her to give him my number and she wouldn't, but she did take his number and gave me the message of his desire for me to call him. She gave me the message with her commentary of, "Don't be no damn fool, but I'm going to give you this message because I promised him and God that I would." I played with the number for a few weeks. Half of me wanted to see him, and I wanted him to see the kids, but most of all that promise that I made as a childhood still reigned in my head.

I had consulted nearly the entire family including my father and they all agreed it was not a good idea. I was just starting to get on my feet and I wasn't 100% but I was well on my way.

Against everyone's will I finally called him. After all, my son had called 911 asking for his dad. Aunt A wanted to kill him and me because in those days they charged for stuff like that. I called him and we talked on the phone forever, and he was telling me how much he missed the kids and I, but he understood that I wasn't coming back to Georgia, so he wanted to come to Texas to see us. I couldn't believe it; he had never really been out of the bounds of Georgia and Florida that I knew of unless it was work related.

He told me he was coming on a bus, since I took the car that was in both of our names and that all he needed was a ride from the bus station. Hindsight is always 20/20, that was a clue that I missed.

At the time, I was working multiple jobs and the kids were in school and then went to a 24 hour daycare afterschool. I was super busy and my life was super structured which is just what my son needed, structure. We had a great routine going and all was going well.

I took off from work to go and get "Derrick" from the bus station even though my family was adamant about me not doing it. I didn't take the kids with me to get him as I wanted to surprise them. Little did I know I would be the one getting surprised.

I was not familiar with Houston as I had not long before moved to Texas, but I will say that the ride to the bus station was one of the longest one hour rides ever. In my head, I could just hear my family telling me, "Don't do it Lolo, nothing good can come from this!" I remembered that my son was now talking real words and was even trying to put together full sentences and how proud I was of that. I thought of, again, that childhood dream of mine and how I was breaking my promise that I made to God when I walked away. Then I was wondering how did "Derrick" find me and could this mean that he really does want to be with me and that even though I had put on weight having his children, he realized I was a good girl? So many thoughts were running through my head but I chose to play it cool and safe.

I got to the bus station and my heart began to flutter, my eyes began to sting, and my head began to swim with a million and one thoughts that were racing to be first. He walked towards the car and I began to hold my breathe because I wanted my emotions to make a decision about how they felt, but that didn't work. He got in the car and we greeted each other as though we were old friends. I am sure that we both probably felt the same mixed emotions.

It was a long silent drive back home, with a little small talk here and there but nothing substantial. I was trying to fill him on the progress of the kids before he got to them. I assured him that I hadn't said anything bad to the kids about him; actually he was rarely a topic of conversation so he had nothing to worry about.

Finally, we got back home. We went and picked up the kids from daycare and took them home. The kids too seemed as though they had mixed emotions, but as with any kid, they were glad to see their father. I sat to the side and watched and did my best not to intervene on their time.

When we got back to the house I cooked some dinner and we all ate. Before we knew it, bedtime had come and "Derrick" bathed the kids while I cleaned the kitchen and we put them to bed. We went back into my bedroom and he began to talk to me and tell me how big he thought the kids had gotten and how proud he was at my son's progress. That was just the affirmation that I needed. Needless to say one thing led to another and we became intimate. This was the best sex that we had in years. I didn't know what else to do but go to sleep; I was exhausted, emotionally drained and sexed up very well. I thought we were both tired, but I guess not.

I woke up the next morning ready to start my day. It never dawned on me that my bed was empty. I did my usual. I got up and showered and got myself together first and then got the kids together.

After I finished getting me together, I went into the other room to wake the kids up and get them together and that's when it hit me, "Derrick" was gone. I had no idea where he could be as he didn't know anything about Texas at all. I was on a time constraint so I went ahead and got the kids together and prepared for the day, thinking he would walk in at any moment.

Before I knew it everyone was ready to go and start our day as usual. I went outside and realized that my car was gone. I was confused and baffled. I called "Derrick's "phone and he answered. I urged him to hurry back as I had to get the kids to school and I had to go to work. That is when he informed me that he was on his way back to Georgia and was already almost through Louisiana.

"What?" How could he do such a thing, I thought to myself? What was I to do now? That was the only car that I had! He didn't seem a bit concerned or remorseful of his actions.

I called my cousin to come and take my kids to school. I called off from work and went to go pick up my check. When I finished that, I went to a used car lot and told the man about my position and what just happened. All I had was my rent money which was about two hundred dollars that I paid every two weeks to my landlord.

The dealer told me that for the two hundred, he could put me in a car but it wouldn't be pretty. I told him I didn't care how it looked; I had kids to take care of and jobs to get to. I just needed a "point car" meaning a car to get me from point A to point B and back. He sold me an old Toyota Corolla station wagon that you had to start from under the hood. I looked at him really funny, but I was desperate. I needed a car. I gave him my rent money and left with a car.

When the rental office opened, I was the first one there to tell them my situation thinking that they would work with me seeing as I had never missed a payment, nor been late. I told the landlord, who was like a mother to me, what happened and I told her that I would pay double my next payday. She told me, "No, it doesn't work that way dear! I told you not to fool with him, but you didn't listen so now you are just going to have to figure it out."

I was stunned! I never thought that she would do this. I knew I couldn't ask any of my family for the money because they were all broke. Not that I didn't try, but I went to my family and told them my issue and I even proposed options to them. Can I borrow $200 for two weeks or can the kids and I come and stay for two weeks? You wouldn't believe the responses I got.

Aunt A told me, "No because I told you not to rush and leave here anyway, and I also told you not to be fooling with that boy!"

Aunt B, who lived across the street from Aunt A, said, "Baby I'm sorry I don't have any room, nor do I have any money!"

They were my only hope. I had no idea what I was going to do but I knew I had to figure out something quick because it was almost time for my kids to get out of school and I had no money for daycare which meant that I would have to get them myself. I sat in my car at the man-made pier and screamed to the top of my lungs.

"How could I be so stupid? Why didn't I just listen to what everyone else told me, and I would still have a car?" I asked myself, "—Was this planned all along? Who put him up to this? He would never do anything like this on his own?" No answers came to my questions, but then I had a solution.

As I sat there on the dike (man-made pier), I realized it was a quiet place and not many people were there all the time, especially at night. "That's it", I thought to myself. My kids are young and a little naïve. I rushed to pick the kids up from school and I told them that we were going on a vacation.

The first thing that my talented and gifted kid said was, "What about school, Mom?" I knew then that she was my child for sure.

I said well school is almost out, there were only a few days left so she would go to school during the day but she couldn't tell her teachers about our vacations that we took at night because the teachers would get jealous and be sad. My son wasn't talking too much those days, so I didn't have to worry about him telling.

I had packed some clothes for them in the car and we went to the dike and slept there for the night. The next day we got up and went to the gas station and cleaned ourselves up and prepared for our day. Thank God for free breakfast and lunch at school.

I knew this was a temporary solution for a temporary problem, but it was the best that I could do at the moment. I had no idea what I was going to do, but I knew that I couldn't miss work.

I dropped the kids off at school and headed to my job at the grocery store. I was a cashier there and had been there for a while. I had never missed a day, so for me to call out the day before everyone knew something had to be wrong. Everyone asked the same question, "What happened to you yesterday?" My response was always, "I had a few issues I had to iron out."

Finally, I was in the break room and just in a daze trying to figure out what I was going to do about my living situation. I couldn't do the dike thing for two weeks, and my family wasn't on my side at the moment. Just then a guy who had been very nice to me at work came in and sat there for a while.

He began to talk to me and of course I was not listening because I was lost in my own thoughts. He told me a joke as he always did every day, but this time I didn't respond. Honestly, I didn't even hear him I was so lost in my thoughts. He tapped me and asked me what was wrong as I was sitting there and tears was coming from my face and I wasn't even aware of it. I looked at him in his eyes and saw, what I interpreted to be, care.

I finally broke down and told him what had happened and he was so upset. "How the hell could a nigga do some shit like that?" I begged him to keep it down and not say anything because I had to figure it out and had yet to do so. He said, "Figure it out? What is there to figure? You all are coming to stay with me!"

"Really?" I cried.

"Yes really! I don't have anything but efficiency, but you all can take the bed and I will take the couch" is what he said.

I was so relieved! I didn't know what to do. I promised him that I would be out as soon as we got paid the next time and I promised that I would keep my kids out of his hair and off his nerves. I told him that we would really only come there to sleep and to bathe, we would do everything else outside of the house.

"Stop Lolo, my house is yours for as long as you need!" he said.

I thanked him again as I ran to the time clock to clock back in. The whole time while I was checking, he was my sacker for the rest of the night and we continued to talk about the arrangements. The more he talked the better I felt.

Shelter—check!

I went to my night job which was at Burger King which made it easier to feed my kids dinner since I couldn't afford daycare; they had to go to work with me. Luckily one of the cool managers was there that night and I explained to her that I didn't have a baby sitter for the night and I didn't want to call in again so I just brought them with me and if she had to send me home I understood. We were already short staffed so she said I had to stay and that she would have her sister who was her babysitter come and pick up my kids and keep them for the night.

What? What was happening here? Could it be that I could talk her sister into helping me out for the next two weeks? It couldn't hurt to ask so I did.

When I went to pick the kids up from her sister's house that night, I noticed that the sister had a house full of kids. I told her a little bit about my situation and she told me that she would watch my kids for two weeks for $100 dollars in food stamps since I didn't have cash. I did have stamps, but no cash, so I agreed. I gave her my food stamp card and we now had a deal.

Babysitter—check!

I felt like I could fly at this point. In one day I now had a place to stay and a baby sitter and I had a car, even if I did have to start it up under the car.

Transportation—check!

I felt like I was back in business. I wanted to call and tell "Derrick" so bad, "You thought you did something, but guess what, we still good!" However, I had nothing to say to him. I was still livid.

After getting the kids from the babysitter and taking them back to our new temporary place, I sat down and reevaluated my schedule so that I could tell the babysitter when I needed her. I noticed Elvin looking at me in my peripheral vision. He asked me what I was doing and I told him. He said, "Hey I will be glad to watch them sometimes since you are working all these jobs." I can even pick them up from the babysitter since she just stays right around the corner and I can have them clean and in bed by the time you get off."

I couldn't believe that this man was being so nice to me and my kids. I felt as though I owed him everything, but I had nothing to give. Things seemed great for about a week. We all worked together as a team. I would drop the kids off at the babysitter on my way to work now that school was out. Elvin would pick them up whenever he got off and they would all hang out at the park and play for a while and then he would take them home and make sure they were clean and in bed by the time I got home. This all seemed so perfect and everything was working out…until!

One night I was super exhausted as I was pulling fifteen to eighteen hour days at multiple jobs trying to recover from this mishap that I had. This night things just seemed different. When I got home Erwin was watching TV and the kids were already in bed asleep. I sat on the couch and did all I could to keep from falling asleep right there. Then it happened!

He reached over and kissed me! I was stunned! I never knew he was even attracted to me like that. I felt that it was the least I could do after all he was doing for me and my kids, so I slept with him. I thought this was a one-time affair but it turned into a nightly occurrence. I told him I didn't want to do it, but I felt obligated and I thought that would make him feel some type of way and not ask for it anymore. That didn't happen. After five nights of this, he told me one day as I was preparing my kids' stuff for the next day that he was tired of the old pussy and he wanted new pussy. I wasn't sure what that meant until his eyes met mine and I saw him look at my daughter. Now it was time to fight. I looked at him and broke down crying. I begged him saying please tell me you haven't done that. I immediately went and grabbed my babies with tears in my eyes and rage in my heart.

"Hell naw, I ain't done no shit like that, bitch is you crazy?" he said.

I begged and pleaded, "Erwin please tell me you didn't, I will do anything just don't touch my babies!"

At that moment the trust between us was broken. I went back to my family and asked to come and stay there for two days and I got the same response. I never told them about the rape because I feared they would take my kids or again tell me I put myself in that predicament so I kept that part to myself. No one would help me!

I proceeded to call my father and his wife and ask them if they could help me. They lived all the way in another city so I asked them could the kids stay there with them for a spell so that I could work some overtime and get established better. Again, I didn't tell them how bad it was, but I didn't feel like I needed to, after all, my step sisters and brothers took their kids there all the time with no problem. Do you believe they told me no as well? Now I am pissed! Mad at the world was an understatement. I knew now I had to take matters in my own hands. This nigga was not even going to get the opportunity to touch my kids, neither of them. I packed all of our stuff and put it in the car.

The kids were sleep so I checked them while they were knocked out and it seemed as though they had been untouched. I went to the babysitter and asked if she had noticed anything and she said, "No, they seem happy with him and he seems to love them."

I left and went to the beach and sat there for a while and really began to beat myself up for all that had happened.

I began to drive back to home and I saw a strip club there on the highway. I needed money and I needed it now. I pulled over to go to the strip joint and saw how crowded it was. I went inside and asked to speak to a manager. I took the manager outside and told him a little about my situation and asked him if he had anything that I could do. I told him that I was not really comfortable going nude as I had a huge cut going down my stomach from having my kids. He looked at me and laughed and said, "There are ways around that baby girl."

I had no clue what that meant, but he let me start off as a waitress. That night I made $71. This was enough to get us a room for the night. The next day I got paid for doing someone's hair, $50. That got me gas and my kid's food. I had two more days before I was getting paid and can move back into my apartment. I needed more than $71. I had talked to some of the girls and they hooked me up with a bathing suit looking lingerie and for two days I was a stripper and made more money in those two days than I got on all of my paychecks from all my other jobs but I knew that was not the life for me and I quit.

After that whirlwind I knew I was really on my own. I could not depend on my friends, though I really had none, and I surely couldn't depend on my family. I was all my kids had and vice versa. I had to come up with a rock solid game plan that involved saving, planning, and being aggressive in what I wanted.

I did just that. I continued on with all of my jobs. I was doing hair, working at Burger King, McDonalds, Whataburger and Sam's Club. I had no time for foolishness. I was all about the paper. The kids only went with me and the baby sitter who was getting paid quite well and ensured that Erwin never came around my kids or me again. I no longer worked at the grocery store so there was no contact between us. I hadn't heard from "Derrick" and personally I didn't care if he rotted in hell. I was on a mission for me and my kids.

This is where more of my problems began to multiply.

Divine Revelation

Through it all, as much as I didn't want to be my mom, we had so many things in common. The biggest commonality is that we were both single mothers, for the most part. We both had one boy and one girl. The biggest difference is that my children developed to be the best friends that I never had. This seems to be wonderful and quite endearing right? Wrong! Of course as they say hindsight is 20/20.

Everything in my life was centered around my kiddos and not just when they were little, but also as adults. I predicated all of my accomplishments on them and how they felt about it. Now this is not all bad, it actually was good for me and I believe that it saved me from a lot of mischief. The problem was that at this point I realized that I had lost myself. If the truth be told I never knew myself to begin with. My relationship with my children further made me dive into Lolo as a mommy and not Lolo as a person.

15

FAILED TO FLOURISHING-RAPE AND SENDING KIDS AWAY

Chapter Foreword

I am healed enough to keep going,
Though at times I want to quit.
I am healed enough to keep going,
Though I know that there are many opportunities that I have missed.
I am healed enough to keep going,
Though I said I couldn't, I wouldn't and I shouldn't.
I am healed enough to keep going,
Though the devil has tried to rip me to shreds and often succeeded because
I fail to seek the face of the God head. Yes I am hurt, but I'm healed. Yes I
bled, but I'm healed. Yes I cried, but I am healed. Yes I tried and failed but
guess what I am still healed and it's in my going that I will be set free from the
long term effects that could consume me. I will remember this trial just for the
testimony. The details won't even matter because all that matters in the end is
the fact that I am healed.

- 365 Revelatory Words for Any Given Day (2017)

The Journey Continues...

———————————— ◆◆◆◆◆ ————————————

Still wracked with guilt of my past errors, I threw myself into and gave all I had to my kids even the more. We were now back into our own place and I was still working like crazy for the summer and now it was time to go back to school. I knew that when school started that I wouldn't have the freedom to work as much as I was because my son would need me and so would my daughter.

This was going to be my son's first year in a regular school and not a special school. I was excited, but I was also scared. When my son first went to school the school had ran a series of test on him to find his proper placement in their facilities.

The best ex-husband was a man who had been after me for a while. We worked together at Whataburger. He was a single man who had his own place. He worked two jobs and was completely self-sufficient. He had watched my struggle and later admitted my ability to pull through it on my own was an attraction to him.

I was on the job when I got the call that my son had been diagnosed as being mentally retarded. I knew he had issues but no one had ever said those words to me. I thought God and I had a pact that he would walk me through this and that I wouldn't be in same predicament of the family that I had visited. Was I being punished for something? Did I do something wrong? Had I not been through enough already and now this?

When I got the call I was in the middle of lunch rush and I just broke down crying. I ran out the door and guess who was right behind me? My best ex-husband! He asked me what was wrong and all I could do was scream and cry. He forced me to calm down and he asked me for my number. I thought that he was using this vulnerable time as a time to step in, but he quickly looked me eyeball to eyeball and said, "It is not about you right now it's about the baby!"

I was floored! No one had ever said those words to me. I finally broke down and gave him my number.

He came over daily and he and my kids would spend a lot of time together. So much so J.J. began to look like him. Finally I was able to get fully back on my feet again. With The best ex-husband's support I was able to regroup and took on a number jobs to get my money back right since "Derrick" had come and turn my world upside down.

When he got back to Georgia, he and his girlfriend concocted up some homemade divorce papers. These papers were trying to change my kids last night to my maiden name. He wanted to give me like $40 a week for child support and a plethora of other foolishness which made me have to go back to Georgia to seek out an attorney and get a divorce filed for real. "Derrick" took me through the ringer the ringer and I couldn't wait to legally get out of it.

Shortly after the best ex-husband and I started dating, my son began to talk for real. He even taught him how to ride a bike. My daughter was the daddy's little girl that I always wanted to be. The similarity was that she was a daddy's girl to her stepdad just like me.

It wasn't long before I felt obligated to make the best ex-husband my husband. I called myself having a surprise wedding for him as he was a man who had never been married and never had any kids. I had set everything up and it was supposed to be a perfect day. He had proposed to me and I had accepted so I didn't think that there would be any problems. Wrong!

His sisters thought completely differently. They made a huge stink about the whole thing. I had sent the best ex-husband to the store while I went in the restroom and changed clothes. I couldn't even get dressed good because there was such a battle between the families. His family felt as though I wanted him for something other than love. They thought it was money but the truth of the matter is that I made more money than he did.

When The best ex-husband got back and heard the mayhem that was going on, my knight and shining armor came to my rescue and said that he was game for the wedding and to proceed whether his sister's liked it or not.

No one had ever stood up for me like that. Even though he came to the rescue, I couldn't enjoy the day because there was so much in my mind.

The pictures from that day showed it. I was in the process of closing on my house when all of this took place and for moment I was in a huge one bedroom apartment.

Within a matter of weeks we moved into a larger apartment. We stayed there for a while and then we moved into the home I had purchased. It was a huge 6 bedroom, three bath home with a two car garage. This was huge for me because I did something on my own that my mother had never done. In fact I was the first of my cousins to purchase a home. I was floating on cloud nine. Even more so, I felt that this was my way of showing my family that I could make it, even without their assistance.

After a while insecurities began to creep in. The home was in my name and at the onset of every argument was that fact. I didn't know what else to do. I wasn't really enjoying life any longer. The best ex-husband and I began having problems. I was on the road singing and preaching and he was the stay at home dad even though he did still work.

Reality slowly began to sink in that I wasn't really happy and I wanted more. I didn't really want to leave my husband because we made one hell of a team, but I also knew what I wanted. I guess you can say I wanted to have my cake and eat it too. Yep, you guessed it. I cheated! I found some man in the church, a new preacher and I would help him write sermons and he would cheer me on when I was up to sing my songs and it just happened and I didn't fight it.

After a short time, I told the best ex-husband about it and we went and talked to the Pastor about it. My Pastor, who I had seen as a true father figure to me, was so disappointed in me. As if I didn't feel guilty enough. After all, it wasn't like the best ex-husband wouldn't do his damnest to give me anything I wanted and/or needed. I was so overwhelmed with guilt, I left the relationship. I wanted to climb in a shell and live there.

Due to the guilt I finally filed for my divorce from the best ex-husband. We still attended church together and all, we were still great friends, I just couldn't get past that mistake. I knew that he was too good of a man to receive that treatment.

It just so happened that Pastor was preaching a series on forgiveness and he kept preaching and preaching and preaching about it. Finally, one Sunday I was in my feelings about the whole the best ex-husband situation and I knew God was trying to move me forward, but I just wasn't ready to budge for some reason. Just then as I was sitting in the choir stand after singing and I reached down in my purse to get a cough drop and when I pulled my hand back out my ring was on my finger. I broke down crying and ran to the altar. When Pastor asked what I came for, I told him that I came to ask my husband for forgiveness for my infidelity, and I wanted him to come and put the ring back on my finger. You would have thought that the best ex-husband had just heard his name on the Price is Right the way he came sprinting and crying down that isle to get his wife back. It was one of the most moving moments ever in my life. There was not a dry eye in the place.

The church helped us to plan a real wedding in the church. It was beautiful. It was the first time I had a real wedding in a church with pictures and family and all of the works. I wish I could say that this happiness lasted forever. Keep reading because the plot thickens!

Divine Revelation

Forgiveness is one of the biggest factors in our life lessons. Oftentimes when we hear the term forgiveness, we often think of the act of forgiving someone else. However difficult that may be, I have found that self-forgiveness can be even more difficult. Though the best ex-husband was ready and willing to forgive me for my indiscretions, every time I looked at him I saw my mistake. I knew that he was a good man, but it didn't take away the shortcomings that he possessed that were really important to me. I later realized that our issues were not just in my lack of ability to forgive myself, but also for me to stand up for myself and walk in the truth of what I needed and desired from a man that The best ex-husband did not possess.

16

FROM CONTENT TO CONFUSED- THE BEST EX-HUSBAND AND "MY FIRST WOMAN"

Chapter Foreword by My best ex-husband

My marriage to Lolo was far from perfect, but I never thought it would end the way that it did. I asked myself why and what was the reason even though I knew that I wasn't mature nor, much of a talker. When Lolo met "My first woman", I was hurt. Before I knew that they were an item, my only concern for Lolo was that she be safe and careful.

When Lolo made her decision I was angry and frustrated with her, and unfortunately I took it out on the kids by not spending time with them anymore and to this day I regret that decision on my behalf. One thing that I never regretted was the relationship that Lolo and I had because, if nothing else it forced me to grow up and be the man that I am today.

Now, I tell Lolo, "Thank you for allowing me to go through what I went through to become who I am." Because of her I can honestly say that we are in a much better place now since we are friends. I will always love, respect and protect her and I bless the honor that she still carries my last name even if it is for business purposes only.

The Journey Continues...

The second marriage for the best ex-husband and I lasted much longer that the first one and though it was a second union, I realized that we never rectified many of the issues from the first.

It wasn't long before I grew discontent with our relationship. I was tired of the same fight on a different day. I would try various ways of making me happy like fostering a close relationship with one of my mom's other sisters names Aunt L.

She would come over on weekends and help with the kids while I traveled singing and preaching and the best ex-husband worked. I would talk to her about everything. She was the closest that I came to having a mom.

She had some alcohol issues, but no matter what she loved my family. She was the one who would always talk to me and tell me all the reasons why I should stay with the best ex-husband, but also why it was okay for me to be angry with Aunt B and Aunt A for what they had done in the past seasons to me and my kids.

By this time I was also in college as well so my schedule was overloaded to say the least. No matter what though, I would still go and get Aunt L every weekend and bring her over for our time together. One weekend, I had gotten a call from Aunt B that said not to go and get Aunt L because she was in the house drunk and would not answer the phone, so Aunt B said that she would go and get her and bring her to my cousin's house for a Mother's Day brunch that she was hosting

I got to the house and it was explosive. My Aunt A and Aunt D had gotten into the worst fight ever (only God knows what it was about, I'm sure something stupid.) I kept trying to call Aunt L to give her the scoop, but she wouldn't answer the phone. I was already mad because Aunt B had never gone to get her saying, "She probably in there drunk and I don't feel like dealing with it. I was so angry, but what could I do? We were already over an hour away from her and the brunch had already started. It was a great time other than the spat between my aunts, the cousins and I always had a great time when we were together but I couldn't keep Aunt L off my mind.

For days I kept trying to call and somehow I knew something wasn't right. I remember that I was at home doing homework and listening to Mary J. Blige's song, "Give Me You." For some reason this song was on repeat. The kids were at school and the best ex-husband was at work. The phone rang. It was Aunt B. I was still angry with her for not bringing Aunt L and I started not to answer the phone but something made me do it. I wish I hadn't because what she was calling to tell me, I didn't want to hear.

"Lolo is the best ex-husband there?" She asked.

"No, he's at work?" I stated.

"Where are the kids?" she asked?

"They are at school, what's up with all the questions?" I asked.

"We over here at Aunt L house and we found her dead!" Aunt B reported.

I dropped the phone and took off running. I grabbed my keys and headed to her house which is normally about a thirty minute drive, but I did it in much less time than that. I remember getting there and half the family was inside and the other half was outside. I don't even remember putting my car in park before I jumped out and headed towards the stairs. I couldn't believe it. I had to see it for myself.

My oldest cousin grabbed me before I could get to the steps and said I couldn't go in until I had calmed down. I hollered and screamed and even though he was bigger than me I felt I could take him down to get to the love of my life, the only lady that I was close to. My other cousins came and helped to calm me down. Finally, they let me in.

The Coroner was there doing his thing. The only thing I was able to see was her foot before they put us all out again so that they could gather the body in the bag and bring her out.

I remember sitting at the bottom of the stairs crying like a mad woman. My heart was hurting so bad. All I could think of was how I was going to explain this to my kids? They brought her out and I remember feeling super lightheaded, super angry and extra inquisitive. I had questions that I needed answered. When they put her in the car and closed the door that opened my mind.

The questions began to flow. How did this happen? Where was she? What could possibly be wrong? Was there foul play involved? Did someone break in? Who did this? Why didn't she call me? The questions were limitless.

We all went back inside. As I sat down on the couch all I could do was sit there and look in the next room and know that in there is where all of my answers were, but I couldn't bring myself to go in there. All I could see was her bed, a coffee table that she had at the foot of her bed and there was a step stool on top of it that was flipped over. What was that about?

Aunt B was talking and telling us what she had found when she came in. Her theory was that Aunt L was standing on the step stool to change the light bulb and fell. By the way that she was laying, that story could be true, but it just didn't feel right to me. This mystery haunted me for the longest time. The police had ruled out foul play because Aunt B had given them her theory and I guess they took that and ran with it. Because Aunt L had been in the house for about four days dead, her body was already in too bad of shape for us to have an open casket at her funeral. This outraged me because I knew that I would never get any closure. It wasn't until then that I realized how important closure was.

We went back home and life just never seemed the same. I can honestly say now that I probably changed tremendously. I never wanted to be home because Aunt L had a room in our home and our home was filled with so much of her. The love and the laughter that she shared with my family remained present and brought pain instead of peace.

I started becoming more active in the church and this is when I met my all-time best friend. We had so much in common. She had just moved to Texas from Missouri, I had not long moved to Texas from Georgia. She had a set of fraternal twins, a boy and a girl and I had my daughter and my son. I was married and so was she except her husband was away and I didn't know about him until much later. She was also the bus driver for the school that all of our family's kids went to. She was and still is my angel, but we had just met not long before I made the decision to leave the best ex-husband again.

The best ex-husband and I were fighting over every little thing. I now know that it was all my fault because the underlying issue was that I didn't want to be home in the house that was now so empty without Aunt L. The best ex-husband and one of my cousins worked at Whataburger. Supposedly the best ex-husband had started this vicious rumor that I wanted him for his money and his credit cards. What? No way!

I don't remember how I found out about it but it got back to me and that was the final straw. I knew that I was doing everything within my power to make him look like the man he was not. I never dishonored him. However, after hearing this lie I felt I had to avenge myself so I let it all out. I let the streets know that in fact I made way more money than he did. I told them of how he couldn't drive even though I had a number of cars which is why he was always on the bike. I went on and on and then I went and found me an apartment and a new church. I wanted nothing to do with him or anyone who knew him. I was so angry not only at the best ex-husband, but at the lack of closure that I had and living on the same street with my family was more than I could bear.

The best ex-husband left for work one day and I called my best friend, and I got my kids out of school early and while he was at work, I packed up and left. I didn't take much except what I could fit into my two bedroom apartment. I left him in the huge house that I had worked so hard for, on the street with my family that who I felt was deceitful, and I moved to my two bedroom apartment where there was peace and no memories of Aunt L. Finally, my kids and I could move on without memories of her all over the place. Little did I know that I was about to make more memories that I couldn't bear to face.

When the best ex-husband got home and realized that we were gone. He immediately called my phone and began asking a number of questions like why did I leave. I had no problem telling him what I knew at the time, which was that I wasn't happy with him, I wasn't happy in that house, I didn't appreciate the lies that he and my cousin concocted up and I just couldn't take it anymore.

He knew that he still loved me and I him, and he couldn't and wouldn't stay away from the kids and I know I didn't want that anyway. I loved the relationship that he had with my kids and he had been around forever and was an amazing dad to them. I continued to encourage and foster the relationship between the best ex-husband and my kids and that worked out for me because I was still able to hit the road and travel with my singing.

One night the best ex-husband and I had a talk and he told me his theory of fixing my life. He told me that he thought if I found some local friends that I would stay home more and perhaps I would be happier. I didn't want to be close to anyone anymore because it was just too much to handle. I had just bought another car and when I came off the road I realized that I needed to do some things to bring it into compliance. I was not familiar with what all I needed to do and I was too tired to ride around or do the research to figure it out.

I drove around the corner to the local mechanic and told her my issue and she told me all that I needed to do. I asked her if I could leave my car for her to take care of, and if she would take me back home so I could sleep while she worked and she agreed. That ride home changed my life forever. Simple chit chat with a stranger turned into simple chit chat that would utterly confuse my life for days and years to come.

She asked me a little about myself and I told her a little of my story. Finally, I made it home. She dropped me off and I went inside and crashed, but before I could get out the car she had offered to take me for dinner and drinks that weekend. I accepted the offer and I told her that God was moving quickly because of the conversation that the best ex-husband and I had the night before. She chuckled and we parted.

When she was done with the car, she called and woke me up and let me know it was ready and that she could come and pick me up when I was up and ready, but no rush. When the best ex-husband got home from work I couldn't wait to tell him about what had happened. He seemed happy for me at the moment. Finally, after I had dinner ready, I called her to come and to pick me up so that I could pay her and get my car squared away.

When I went over there to pick up my car she made me wait to pay. While waiting this big lady drove up, apparently this was one of her best friends. She and the lady began to discuss something about my car. I never paid it any real mind, I was just in awe of how tall this lady was and I was trying to figure her out because I had only saw people like her on television. Finally "My first woman" and I had exchanged numbers and I went home.

She called me later that night to see how the car was doing and I assured her all was well. She told me that she couldn't wait for the weekend so we could hang out at dinner. Little did I know our reasoning and anticipation was for different reasons.

The best ex-husband and I had went to dinner the next day and I told him that I had been talking to "My first woman" and all that she was saying to me and he asked me the question, "Is she gay?" I had no idea what that meant. I laughed it off because I never knew that women could be gay. When I told him that, he looked at me and laughed as though he thought I was kidding. I went on to assure him that I had never seen a gay girl before in my life, guys maybe, but never a girl.

I couldn't wait til we got home to call her and tell her what he said. "My husband asked me if you were gay!" I told her.

"Tell him I said, 'Don't be scared!'"

My silly self ran and told him what she said as though we were playing telephone. The best ex-husband looked at me with the biggest question mark but I ignored his bewilderment and continued talking to her. We had frivolous talk until the weekend came.

Finally, Friday was here and it was time to go out. I thought for sure it would be a group of us, especially the big monster lady; I wanted to see her again just so I could stare and try to understand her in some way. It was just "My first woman" and I. We got to the restaurant for the night that changed my life forever.

It seemed like almost immediately the conversation got deep. I like to call the conversation "Lesbianism 101." For the first time in a long time I was in a conversation that literally intrigued me. She finally admitted to me that she was gay. I told her that I had never met a gay woman before to my knowledge, but I assured her that I was strictly dickly and that my stomach could never stomach being intimate with ""My third woman"" in that way.

"Don't knock it til you try it!" she said.

I told her that I have a very weak stomach and that to put my mouth on a woman was out of the question.

"You don't necessarily have to," she told me.

Now I was even more confused. She goes on to give the ins and outs and not once did she make me feel stupid nor did I feel judged for not knowing. I told her that I was learning more about life that night then I had learned in a long time. She was glad to fill me in.

When dinner was over we rode from home down to the beach. My mind was going about 200 miles per hour and I knew that this wasn't intellectually legal. When we got to the beach she asked me if I had any more questions that she could answer and I told her, "Not right now, I'm still trying to take all of that other stuff in. It may take some time for me to digest that let alone ask for any more information. Right about there was where my normal life ended.

I turned my head and she kissed me. Wow! Ding! Oh Lord! She kissed me with such passion and love that there was no way I could turn back. I reciprocated with the same amount of passion that I had received and hands began to move and hormones and emotions began to spark. I didn't even want to go home. I wanted to stay in this moment forever, even though I didn't know what this moment was.

Divine Revelation

I had no idea that so many turns could happen in one season. I went from being a happy mom, wife and niece to my whole world crumbling down all at once. From the death of my aunt to the separation from my husband to trying to change my entire sexual makeup. I wish I could say I traveled this path for this reason or for that reason but I honestly can't. All I can say is that these decisions were a part of my journey and that it changed the course of my life for a significant amount of time.

SEXUAL WHIRLWIND-ALL THE LADIES

Chapter Foreword by My daughter

When my mom made the transition from loving a man to being intimate with a woman, it was a huge life change. It gave me a different perspective on traditional relationships, roles, and life in general. I was in middle school at the time so it made life confusing as hell. So not only was my mother confused so was I.

Usually my brother would come to me for the answers, but in this period of time I had none and it bothered/angered me because I couldn't go to my mom because she was busy catering to this woman who wanted to be a man. This began my anger period in my life.

I was angry at my biological father for not being there, my stepfather for not fighting or just letting us go, and my mother for dragging us through this. My relationship with "My first woman" was all hate on the outside and a little aww on the inside.

I say that because I was seeing her do things that I was told a man was supposed to do, but I had never seen a man do. We didn't want or need for anything that I know of, besides our own rooms so we didn't have to listen to them have sex. This started my brother on his touchy feely phase that I had to deal with for years. When "my first woman" and mom broke up I thought it was over but little did I know it was just the beginning and little did I know that I would grow to appreciate "my first woman".

Chapter Foreword by my son

When my mom left the best ex-husband and went with "my first woman" I was confused and did not really accept it. I became used to it as I got to know "my first woman" more. However, when she got to """My third woman""", that was the most painful time for me, especially when I went to stay with her and she was physically abusive to me. Nevertheless as with all obstacles that we endured and came through together as a family, we treated that no differently. I was so glad that my mom took the time not just for her to heal, but for all of us to heal.

The Journey Continues...

"My first woman"

It wasn't long before "My first woman" and I had gone all the way. When that finally happened, I stopped sleeping with the best ex-husband completely. I can't explain it. He was still my husband but I didn't want to cheat on "My first woman". I knew that she would know if I had slept with him or not, so I just played it safe. I would jump and run every time the best ex-husband tried to touch me. I knew that what I was doing was wrong but I couldn't explain the rationale behind my loyalty to "My first woman".

By this time I had graduated college in the small city and had to move to the larger city to continue my education. I was terrified of the larger city and its traffic and everything else about it. It was a bit overwhelming to me; however "My first woman" knew it like the back of her hand and was not intimidated by any of it.

She had a place in the larger city with her ex-girlfriend who was moving out, so "My first woman" came up with the great idea of us moving in that apartment together. It was nearing the end of the school year and the ex-girlfriend didn't want to move her son from his school so late in the year. We could understand that so the little boy stayed with us until school was out and my children stayed with the best ex-husband for the same reason. For that season, it was just "My first woman" and I. I had pretty much stop attending my church because that was our day to rest as we had established our own little routine.

Mondays thru Thursdays we worked and I did my school work. Fridays was our date night where we would go and paint the town red in our own way. Saturdays was our night that we hung out with our lesbian friends, and just had a blast, and Sundays we rested and prepared for the next week. This went on until school was out and then I brought my kids with me and the ex-girlfriend came and got her son.

I still was not sure how to explain to my kids this phase of my life. I wasn't even sure of what was going on myself. How could I explain something that I myself didn't understand? "My first woman" had no children, so she was no help in that department of explaining it to the kids.

Finally one Saturday I sat them down and told them the truth of who she was. I told them that she was more than a roommate, she was my girlfriend. My son laughed because he had no clue what I was talking about and my daughter just looked at me as if to say, "What?" If I had never been exposed to lesbians myself, surely they had no clue what was going on.

It was so interesting because on this particular weekend lifetime was playing all these movies about same sex relationships and we all sat down and watched them as though we were in class. Of course they were movies that were scripted, but they did give us a bit more exposure to the life that none of us had a clue about but I found myself in.

When "My first woman" got off we would alternate our activity weekends, one weekend we would do something as a family and the other weekend we would do something for us. This was heaven for me. Finally, I was able to go somewhere I didn't have to drive. I was actually getting out and enjoying life, spending the fruits of my labor. For the first time I was working as a team. We never needed or wanted for anything. If I didn't have it, "My first woman" did and vice versa.

It took a while, but the kids had become accustomed to our new life and were coming to enjoy it as well. I had no idea what was going on inside of their little bodies. I knew that they really liked "My first woman" and that adoration began to manifest itself because they began acting like her. She was the stud (male) in the relationship so she always dressed the part and this was a way for my daughter to become comfortable being the tomboy she was and my son just stayed in his own world so nothing ever fazed him, so I thought.

Our new normal was established and we continued our lives as normal people. I was so happy and then I started to notice that there was a separation that was taking place between "My first woman" and I. She began to start going to hang out by herself. There would be times that she said that she was going with her family and since they didn't accept her lifestyle I was not invited. I knew something was going on but I couldn't put my finger on it. I felt the shift in our relationship but I didn't know how to fix it because I was so new to the lifestyle.

This was the beginning of me losing myself. I started drinking more. I started smoking. I wasn't going to church. I was barely talking to church folk. I had alienated myself from family and friends because I didn't want them to ask me questions that I had no clue how to answer so I just stayed away. I figured somehow I would work through this on my own.

"The Other Woman's" friends became my friends and I had made new friends as well. I began to lean on them to a certain extent for support because again I had no idea what I was doing. Then they even began to distance themselves from me.

One day "My first woman" had gone to "run an errand" and I didn't question it because this had become a norm. I didn't even ask to go because I knew what the answer would be. Then all of a sudden the telephone rang. I answered and it was "My first woman". She told me to stay inside and not to answer the door because her ex-girlfriend was following her home and she was telling all manner of lies about her. I was so confused but one thing that I wasn't was a punk, I hadn't forgotten how to fight to defend me and mine, so I put my tennis shoes and head scarf on and I was ready for whatever. I went outside and waited for them to come around the corner to our parking lot. I didn't know what to expect but I told my kids to lock the door and not to open it for no one but "My first woman" or myself. They were watching TV so they were not alarmed at all.

While I was standing outside looking from the balcony, I saw them interacting with each other. They exchanged words a few times, one minute "My first woman" was coming upstairs, then the next minute the girl was coming up, but neither of them ever made it so I went down and asked if there was something that she wanted to say to me. Both of them looked shock to see me. I assured them I have been a lot of things in my life but a punk was not one of them and I am not never been a scary cat.

She assured me that her beef was not with me, but with "My first woman" because apparently they had been messing around and she had asked "My first woman" for some money and she refused to give it to her so she was threatening to come and tell me about their affair.

"My first woman" assured me that the girl was lying and since I was completely sold out to her, I wanted to believe that she was completely sold out to me as well. I chose not to believe the girl, even though the times that she told me that they were together lined up with the times that "My first woman" was missing in action with me. My loyalty overrode my rationale about the situation.

When the girl saw she wasn't getting anywhere she left and "My first woman" and I went on the balcony and began talking. She again tried to assure me that the girl was lying and was just jealous of the relationship that she and I had. She told me about the blackmailing part and all and I bought it, however, our relationship was never the same. Even though she had taken me into the house and sexed me like never before and then took me shopping and we went on our way to enjoy the rest of our day.

The apartment that "My first woman" and the ex-girlfriend had was a one bedroom on the third floor. Now that my kids were here we needed more space so we moved into a two bedroom, two baths in the same complex. This apartment was in just "The Other Woman's" name and now there was no way that this girl could find us again and do any further damage to our relationship.

Of course, as with all relationships with infidelity, "My first woman" and I were stuck together like glue for a season. I knew where she was at all times and vice versa. I never really did anything but go to work and go to school and then I was back at home playing wife and mom, cooking and cleaning and taking care of the kids. My confusion was now manifesting itself as anger and resentment. "My first woman" thought that it was about her and the ex but in reality now looking at hindsight it was all about the battle within me.

When we moved to the new apartment on the second floor of another building, I thought that this would be the sign of a new beginning for us, but in reality it wasn't. It was a new spot with the same issues. "My first woman" began to stray again. I had no evidence but I had a really strong instinct that she was cheating, but I had no proof. She even told me that she had taken this night job at Wal-Mart. I thought this was weird because we were not in need of any money or anything. We were both working and splitting the bills down the middle for the most part and we had enough left to still have fun. However, again I didn't question it.

The abandonment had gotten to be too much and I had caught "My first woman" in a lot of lies including this night job situation. I knew now I had to find myself again and put the focus back on me and my kids. I had to come up with a plan. I didn't know what this plan was, but I knew that I had to create one. I was stressing with school, work, raising my kids, the best ex-husband was tripping about spending time with them and they could feel it, my drinking and smoking was getting out of hand, but I still felt as though I had control.

Then hurricane season came and Hurricane Katrina had hit New Orleans. This was a major turning point in my life. Hurricane Katrina was a physical devastation for the refugees, but it was a spiritual metaphor for me. Those people were fleeing from the devastation of the water from the storm and I was fleeing from the crying at night that I was doing because I was confused. They had household damage from the hurricane and my household was damaged because my kids were just as confused as I was about the whole homosexual matter. Both of them now thought that this was normal and was trying to experiment on their own with their own sexuality. This is what made me experience a song entitled, "I Told the Storm!" The song was in heavy rotation on the radio and the exposure was great, but I was living this song more than performing it. However, this did provide me with an opportunity to create a better life for my children and me.

The song had a much deeper meaning for me;

Lyrics	Revelation
Winds stop blowing...	Stop telling me lies
Floods stop flowing...	I have to stop crying over this matter
Lightening stop flashing...	No more shocks of infidelity
Breakers stop dashing...	I will no longer be overwhelmed by this
Darkness go away...	I have to educate myself or move on
Clouds move away...	Sex will no longer cloud my vision
Death can't shake me...	I will live through this
Job Can't make me...	I was working but doing things that contradicted my conviction making me stay longer than intended
Bills can't break me...	I can make it without child support or her help
Disease can't take me...	I believed God for a clean bill of health
You can't drown me...	I will no longer be overwhelmed by these occurrences

Finally I moved into another apartment with my children alone. I was done with "My first woman". I finally found the strength to break away. So I thought. She still had some furniture at my apartment and her and her ex-girlfriend came to get it. That's right the same one she said she had nothing to do with. I was devastated. This was the worst blow ever. I had to start all over again, but I was more devastated by the blow that she brought this woman to my home that I couldn't function.

I lay in bed and cried for days. I couldn't sleep. I barely ate. My kids were with the best ex-husband for a few days to spend time with him and I didn't have the will to live. I didn't want to sing, I didn't want to travel, quite honestly, I just wanted to lay there and die. I felt like I couldn't breathe. It felt like the wind was literally knocked out of me. This was an emptiness I never felt before, not even when my mother passed.

People would call and I wouldn't answer, come by and I ignored the door. I just felt like life was over. There was no reason to go on. I thought it couldn't get any worse than it was, but boy was I wrong. "My first woman" and I still had the same circle of friends and one of our closest friends was having her birthday party. She insisted that I come and said she didn't believe that "My first woman" was coming so the coast should be clear. I told the best ex-husband about the party and he had agreed to go with me and everyone was on board with that, so I took him as my friend and I had made that abundantly clear to all parties.

We got to the party and my stomach was in knots about the whole situation. Not only was "My first woman" there but she brought her ex-girlfriend and I found out that they were back together and living together and had been for some time. POW!!! The devastation knocked me back into that dark place again.

I dropped the best ex-husband off back to his place and I headed back to home. Then my friends called and told me not to go home, but to come and hang out with them at a club, so I did. I thought that I could handle it especially since "My first woman" was not going to be there. I got there and it was lesbian heaven and the women were all over me. I felt as though this was just what I needed even though on the inside I was still numb and devastated. It was a large group of us there and we were having a good time. I had given my number out to so many females I had no clue who they were when they called. Sad!

"The second woman"

In the midst of our friends was another lesbian named "The second woman". She was a stud as well, but she was sickly. Not sick unto death at the time, but she had some medical issues that caused her not to be able to work. She had just gotten out of a bad relationship herself and we became close friends. She wind up having to leave her apartment and she moved in with me. It was only a matter of time before her daughter and granddaughter came to live with us as well. This was more than I could handle.

She could not stand "My first woman", and I believe that feeling was mutual. They had some past history that I knew nothing about and also that I was not interested in. All I knew was that "the second woman" was a great friend during the time that I needed her most. Yes, we eventually became lovers but I was still operating in my numb state, so I was not fully invested and I couldn't help but wonder if she was with me only to get back at "My first woman".

One day "My first woman" had called and asked could she come over so that we could talk and I told her yes, like a dummy. She came over a little earlier than promised and I was in the bathtub. I let her sit there and talk to me while I took a bath because I knew that there was nothing that she could say that could make me take her back after all the devastation. I was numb, but not dumb.

As she sat there and talked to me, she asked for a key to my place. She didn't know that "the second woman" was staying there as well at the time, but I refused to give her a key. After a while, she got angry and grabbed my purse and took the keys out and ran out of the door. Naked and all I ran out of the door behind her to get my keys. She almost got away until she tripped on her shoes and fell down the curb landing nearly under her car.

At that moment I ran in the house and got a robe and went outside to assist her. Of course I got my keys first, but then I helped her up and took her inside to clean her wounds. Just then "the second woman" called and I told her what happened. She insisted that I just get my keys and send "My first woman" on her way. I couldn't do it. She was bleeding everywhere from the cut on her knees to her hand and even her face.

After I got her cleaned up, I sent her on her way, but then I realized she took the house key off of my keychain. I kept calling her and she wouldn't answer or when she did answer, she refused to bring the key. I had no energy to deal with it, so I told her I was calling the police and I did.

The police came and I made a report. They called her and told her to bring the key back; she had no legal rights to my apartment. I also called my brother and told him what happened. He came over as well. Right when he got there, "My first woman" came in. With the police there my brother looked at her and said, "Damn Lolo, what did you do to her?"

With fear and trembling I assured him and the police that I didn't do it, she did it to herself. All of them gave me the side eye as though they didn't believe me. She actually had to tell them from her own mouth what happened. My brother still didn't believe me because he knew me to be a fighter. She finally gave me my key back and everyone left. I knew then that I had to take some further steps in my life to get away from the drama. My only hold up was school. I was almost done with my bachelor's degree.

After Hurricane Katrina there was Hurricane Rita and she was heading for my city. Now we were refugees, trying to get away from the storm, both literally and metaphorically. I had regained contact with an old friend from high school. She lived in another part of Texas and invited me and my family to come to her house until the storm passed. I was a little leery seeing as though I had never heard of nor been to where she was, but I accepted her offer and I went. It was just my kids, my Aunt D and my cousin.

What was supposed to be a three hour drive turned into a 24 hour drive. Traffic was bumper to bumper, nevertheless, we finally got there. There wasn't enough room for all of us so my kids and I stayed with my friend while the rest of my family went to a hotel. The storm had passed and my family went home but I stayed a few more days so that I could attend church. She told me that her bishop wanted to meet me.

We went to church on Sunday and it was amazing. These people knew nothing about me, yet he spoke life to me and my situation. He told me that their city is where I was supposed to be. I hadn't heard otherwise and everything else that he said seemed to be on point so why should I doubt that he was right that I was supposed to be there.

I went home and prayed and thought, and thought and prayed. Everything at my house was fine but my cousin was without lights so they came over to hang out a bit. I began telling them about my experience at the church and of course they had nothing to say except, "You still got that moving stuff in your blood. You got that from your mama!" We all laughed and I began to do some research and all that it had to offer.

I told "the second woman" that I was leaving and she was going to have to find somewhere to stay. She had met someone online and they moved in together in Dallas. That to me was confirmation that I was free to go especially when I got accepted into a college up there that transferred nearly all of my credits. Find a church, check. Find a school, check. Clear the air here in my old city, check. All I had to do now was go to my new destination and find a job and a place to stay.

One day the Lord impressed it upon my heart to take off from work and drive to my new destination. I wasn't sure why but I did it. I went there with $1000 in my pocket. By the time I left there, I had a home, a job, had registered for school, joined the church and felt as though I was on my way to recovering from all that was "My first woman".

Divine Revelation

This chapter reminded me of a truth that I continued to believe for the longest time. That truth was that right before I graduated; there was always some sort of catastrophe for me. Before I graduated high school, my mom passed away. When I was preparing to graduate with my associates, I was going through a divorce from the best ex-husband. When I was preparing to graduate from my Bachelor's degree I was going through a bad breakup with """"My third woman"""". I was afraid of graduating seasons for a moment but it never stopped my drive for education.

18

JUST NOT SURE-BISEXUALITY

Chapter Foreword by Close confidant

I witnessed Lolo discovering the fluidity of her sexuality. As a Trans person myself, I understand the labels that are placed on us and I believe that Transgenders and bisexuals get the hardest hit of the Lesbian, Gay, Bisexual, Trangender, Queer (LGBTQ) community. Trans are seen as mentally ill and Bisexuals are seen as freaks who just want it all. The truth of the matter is that we are neither.

Lolo is sharing her brave feat of exploring her sexuality. Having to deconstruct the construction of her sexual makeup compounded with religious expectations and confines, I watched and assisted Lolo through her discovery. I held her hand, metaphorically as she went through the fundamental grief, her anger, her denial, and finally her acceptance. The acceptance didn't come easy because you have to overcome the fear and frustration that can make or break your experience.

Unlike others, Lolo did the work. She researched and educated herself and others in the process of her evolution. This has empowered her to make outsiders of the community think and the insiders hopeful of the catalyst of change that she can become.

When I think of Lolo or see her I smile, I pray, I watch and most of all I get excited because I believe that she has the ability to reach the educated as well as the uneducated. She talks to those who have no clue and pushes them to the point of action. She is one who can walk people through their uproot of old beliefs and usher them into new ones without losing sight of the vision and for that I am so Godly proud of her and will always be a friend and an ally. Keep up the good work my friend! You are one step closer to yourself.

Lolo's Confidant

The Journey Continues...

There was a season in my life that I went back and forth with my sexuality. I was the most confused. I would try to do "right" and be with a man. He broke my heart. I flipped to be with a woman and she did me wrong. I went back to men, then women, then men, then women. I played sexual volleyball over the span of some years taking some of that time to be single and get a mental reprieve. I tried every way that I could to meet people, including online dating.

As I went through life, I became more and more confused as to what I wanted, or shall I say who I wanted. One thing that I can say for sure is that I didn't want to bring my sexual confusion into any relationship so I just remained single for a season at times.

I then sought God for real in reference to my sexuality and I didn't really receive an answer. Not an answer that I was convinced I heard anyway, so the saga continued.

2005-2006 Woman ("My first woman")

As you have witnessed in the prior chapter, my initial encounter with a woman was explosive. I loved everything about it. I never wanted for anything. She did everything for me as a woman that I thought that a man should do. We were a true team act. When I didn't have she did and vice versa. She brought balance to my life. She taught me that there was more to life than just work and that if you work hard, you should also play hard. We had date nights every Friday. She balanced out time for just the two of us as well as time with the family and that I loved. However, infidelity got the best of that relationship and I ended it.

2006-2008 Single

After my first relationship with a woman I was worn out. I never thought that it would end. I loved her with love that I didn't even know I had.

I knew after that excursion that I needed a break. I didn't know how to recover from that. I had no idea what "bisexual" was. Now I battled with "what am I supposed to do now? If I go with a man, will he have me? Do I tell him that I was with a woman before? What will he think? How do I explain it? Am I supposed to come out? What does that even mean? Am I gay? Am I straight? Why didn't she teach me this part in our initial conversation when she taught me everything else? She never said what do you do when it doesn't work out. Who can I ask?

With all of these questions I knew I better not take this ball of confusion that I was any further. This is how people get hurt. Due to this confusing personal life, I threw myself into work. I was new to the city and I was trying to recover financially plus I was now in the teacher's program at school and was heavily involved in other activities at school. Not to mention being in the church and upholding my duties there. This allowed me the opportunity to drown my confusion with other things. It worked for a season.

2008-2009 "My third woman"

While in my new city, I was so confused, I decided not to date at all for a season. I wasn't sure whether I wanted men or women so I did neither. I kept to myself and committed to a life of celibacy. I wanted God to give me clarity before I brought my confusion to someone else's life. I stayed single from 2006-2008 and then I decided to try ""My third woman"". I met this woman online. She was so cool. I could talk to her about anything. She was like literally my best friend. She lived away and her name was "My third woman". Again, she was ""My third woman"" who went above and beyond in her relationships, fulfilling what was thought to be the man's job. We started off as friends, but quickly became lovers. She wind up moving with me and we accomplished a lot together.

I was still in college but was no longer traveling nor was I really working because I didn't have to, I was living off the residuals of my music career. When "My third woman" moved with me, I felt I was really on to something. I had experienced some church devastation and had left but now I was back in church or at least trying to get there by visiting and she would join me. She was the most encouraging person that I knew and I felt that together we could do great things.

I had my own kids and she had none but she had a love for kids, at least I thought. The true test came when we became foster parents. We were one of the first same sex couples allowed to foster in our state of Texas. We were a power team. "My third woman" was working at Sprint making decent money, I was in school still living off of royalties and other means of income, my kids were thriving and doing well. We went through a lot of adversity, but we achieved and succeeded. We got foster parents of the year which was major because we were the first same sex couple to achieve such an honor. We didn't have many friends because we were both new to the area and then on top of that our sexuality kept us in seclusion to a degree, especially because I was closeted.

I had introduced "My third woman" as my sister/assistant and for a moment that was fine until she got tired of the lie and wanted to be who she was in the streets as well as in the sheets. I understood but I was not brave enough to step out of my comfort zone just yet.

That issue carried over into our interaction and life together. She began to act different with all the children. There was no permanence in her talk with me anymore. For instance, I would tell her that I loved her and I wanted to be with her forever and she would look at me and say, "Nothing lasts forever, dear." Every time she said that it was like a dagger to my heart. In time, it made me shut down and we were both no good for each other.

She started talking to her ex-girlfriend and that was a reminder of what "My first woman" had done to me, so I was not having that and then low and behold "My first woman" was trying to call and talk to me again. I knew that no good thing could come from this. I asked her to stop talking to her ex and I told her how it made me feel. She refused saying, "She is always going to be my friend!" That was a slap in my face every time she said it. Little did I know that this is where I would start learning what abuse was.

My kids had left to go and see their father for the summer and we were slowly but surely clearing the house of foster children because I think that we both knew that our season was coming to an end. We never spoke it, but it was like inside we just knew. While the kids were gone, I got the call that Aunt A had been hospitalized and it wasn't looking real good. I rushed down to see her and I stayed with my best friend. Before I knew it Aunt A had passed. We were all there when she took her last breath and I thought I was going to lose it, especially because I was singing to her when she passed. This made it extra hard for me.

I remember going back to my best friend's house and completely losing it and "My third woman" called and tried to calm me down, but nothing and no one could help me. She was my last favorite aunt and I couldn't help but think of all do the things she had done for me and my kids. Again, I had to break news of another death to my kids. They rushed home after the news to try and make it for the funeral. Ironically when we buried my Aunt A, we also buried my relationship with "My third woman".

When I got back home I realized that "My third woman" had been entertaining her ex while I was away and that for me was a wrap. I called the police after "My third woman" had an altercation with one of the foster kids which made it easier to clear the house of foster kids. My kids were home now and I was still grieving my aunt. As with any breakup, things got ugly before they got better. "My third woman" had just bought me some appliances and because we were done she came and took the appliances back. Like she literally walked down the street with the appliances one at a time on a dolly in the middle of the night. That is when I knew that we made the right decision.

"My third woman" was the disciplinarian of the house and my son had started acting out so I threatened to send him to stay with "My third woman" for a moment and he continued so I made good on the threat. Something told me one day to go to his school and check on him, which was nothing unusual. This particular day, I got there and it was an eery feeling in my gut. When I laid my eyes on my son I was bewildered by what I saw. He had been beaten. I was livid. I didn't know whether to scream, cry, holler, shoot or pray. All of the above was an option.

I asked my son what happened to him and each time his story changed. I never really got the whole truth, so I went to her place and got all of my babies stuff and brought him home. I was a big ball of emotions. I felt guilt for sending him over there. I felt anger that I could even think that she would do this to him. Even though he never told me that she did it, I just believe in my gut she did. Because he wouldn't tell me I couldn't get the law involved but I knew now what I had to do.

At that point I married myself back to my children. We had all been through some trauma so we all needed a healing period. I was finishing with my bachelors in a few months and I was getting ready to start my masters. My son was acting a complete fool in school and everywhere else. He had just reached a rebellious phase and I felt that it was all my fault for all that I had taken them through with my love life. I chose to chill out on the love thing for a while, so I went back to being single and celibate again.

I focused on my kids, my schooling, my career and my goals which was to go all the way through to my doctorates. I was entering into an exciting time in my life. I was about to graduate school with honors and my dad was actually coming to my graduation. This was the most exciting thing that had happened to me in a long time. He missed my high school graduation for whatever reason. He missed my associate's graduation because of a date mix up between him and his wife I believe, but he was actually planning to travel from his home to mine to come and see me graduate. I was elated. "the second woman" came as well which was a treat but by this time she was really sick and found it not to be robbery to come and share this time with me. I was so grateful. Not to mention that all of my children from my jobs were coming as well. This was a great time for me. Hold on though because it doesn't last for long.

2009 Single

I knew that above all I wanted to be normal again. I was going to a church that at the time of my "deliverance" they seemed obsessed with my sexuality and marital status.

In my mind, I felt like every sermon ended with the homosexuality piece. Every women's meeting began and ended with the sexuality piece. I felt like all services were about why Lolo needed a man. I know it seems petty, and it may not even be true, but that was my feeling. I felt the need to prove that I was no longer gay and the church is what made me feel that I had to do that. I was so frustrated.

2010-Single/Husband #3 (Man)

I then started back to dating men. I remember going on a pre-tour in preparation of the release of my first book, Churchin' Ain't Easy and my first cd, "Can I Just Be Me?" I had a team that was the most gracious to me. They were the family that I never had. They ensured that I stayed relevant and in the market. As I was touring I was also doing my Christian comedy. It was my trademark to never tell the same joke no matter what city I was in.

I allowed my team to talk me in to putting myself out there to win a date within select cities where I was new to the market. That was a huge mistake, but I did it.

I didn't know how to feel about it, but I trusted my team. Well after my radio appearance, the winner was announced. Nationwide they announced the winner. His first name was Husband #3. The first thing that I said when they announced it was the interpretation of his name which is, "God is with us!" Little did I know that those would be my words to live by.

Finally we went on our date. He walked in and I was already sitting down. My security was at another table, so I felt safe. Of course, when he came in I didn't know who he was so they had made the arrangements for the host to bring him to the table when he showed his identification to them.

I'm sitting there and saw them walking him towards me. "Not too bad," I thought. He was little short, but he was dark and handsome. Very debonair and clean shaven. Then he opened his mouth. He was African!

Why I was taking this so personal I wasn't sure, except the fact that I had been scammed for thousands of dollars by Africans but nevertheless, a commitment was a commitment so I didn't run.

He began to tell me about himself and how he was a huge fan. He told me more about myself than I thought any stranger should know. I was the utmost impressed that he had followed me from city to city and enjoyed my comedy shows and was even able to retell a joke or two. As a matter of a joke, I said, "Well dang if you love me like that then we should get married so you will be able to come to all of my shows for a discount." I swear I was only joking. Not funny!

When I returned to Texas on Monday, he was there. He had contacted my team and they got in touch with me and told me of his presence. I was stunned but it didn't seem like such a bad idea. At least this way the church people would get off my back and now they would believe me when I say that I am not gay. The following Sunday I went to church and the Pastor married us in his office. Little did I know that day would change the very course of my life.

Everything was going well at first. He was a chef so he cooked all of the time. I was working and he was looking for work. He asked me one day where the African market was and I told him I was clueless but at the time I was wearing braids that I only allowed the Africans to do so I referred him to them.

Not only did he go to the market for food but for women as well. He became a regular at the market and at the braiding salon. As I went away for shows, he never came with me. When I confronted him about it, he said, "If you would book stuff locally then I could attend!" I called him on his bluff. I had my team to book me some dates locally.

Things around my home was very interesting, to say the least. His drinking was costing me a fortune to the tune of about $300 a week. He was a much more outgoing person than I was. He wanted to have parties all the time or attend them at least. When I wasn't home instead of him looking for work, he was hanging with the African women at other braiding salons than the one I referred him to.

One day I was at home cooking dinner and he was in my bedroom, where my cell phone was located. This was a clear indication that I had nothing to hide. My publicist text me her new number as she was just getting out of a bad relationship. I was the youngest of the team so they all called me "baby girl." The text specifically read, "Baby girl this is my new number, and don't forget the show on Friday." He came into the kitchen and confronted me about the text.

"What the hell is this?" He asked.

I didn't have any glasses or contacts in so I couldn't really see. Before I knew it he had hit me in the head with my own cell phone. I was stunned. So much so that for days I walked around saying, "Did this nigga just hit me in the head with a cell phone"

After days of walking around like that, my team finally took me to the doctor and he told us that I was in a state of shock. He helped me through that state and had urged me to not go home. I had a better plan. Let God deal with him.

Finally it was time for the hometown gigs that he told me to book. I had a full weekend planned and I just knew that I was going to see my husband there. Part of me was excited, and the other parts of me were in turmoil. On top of all of that, I was getting sick. As always, I pushed through and made my appearances. Appearance one, no Husband #3. Appearance two was a parade, I kept calling him to come in the lineup with me, but he never answered. As I rode the parade route, I noticed him on the sidelines with his new guy friend from Africa. Appearance number three, was a comedy show benefit for a battered women's shelter and, you guessed right, no Husband #3 there either.

I was on my way home and I called him and asked him to please make me some soup as I was really sick and just wanted to eat and go to bed. He hollered at me saying, "You are just trying to control me, I am not coming home until I am ready, I may even spend the night with my friend!"

I was livid and didn't know which way was up.

I asked him the question, "What man still has slumber parties in his forties?" He never answered and hung up on me.

Too sick to contend with him, I just had the driver to take me home and I had my kids to make me some soup and I went to bed. As I laid there I thought about the many other occurrences that had happened in this short lived relationship. He had embarrassed me in front of my friends, my family, and my coworkers and now he has the nerve to forsake me while I am sick. I am done!

As the night went on, I was feeling worst and worst. My kids were not driving yet and I needed to go to the emergency room. I called him eleven times and sent him fifteen texts and no response did I receive. Finally, I called my assistant and asked her to come take me to the hospital and while I had the phone in hand, I called my attorney and demanded that he bring me some divorce papers. He laughed and said, "I am an entertainment attorney!"

I responded, "Well I know you know somebody and I need to get this done ASAP!"

Needless to say there were divorce papers delivered to my house by midnight.

The next morning, he came home and after a brief encounter, I told him there was something on the nightstand waiting on him. When I said that, he quickly ran to the night stand with excitement to see what it was, as I was known to be full of surprises. This was the surprise of his life. After reading the papers, he commented, "You didn't even give us a chance!"

Nothing mattered to me anymore I knew I was done.

2010-2013- Single/The Pastor/ "The Musician" (Both)

My first book was released in 2011 so after my divorce in 2010 I was way too busy to be dating plus I needed time to heal. My daughter had graduated high school in 2010 and was going to college; my son had gone to Arizona with his dad while I toured the country with my book. I finally felt like I was being productive again. My book was out and doing well, I had started my Masters and had entered theology school. I had hoped that somewhere in there that I would find some clarity on this sexuality thing.

For once, things were going well again, or so I thought. Then life hit once more. I was robbed and wound up homeless again. This homelessness was really by choice unlike the homelessness that I had encountered before.

After my home had been robbed, I was afraid to stay home anymore and then I didn't want my daughter to be at home alone anymore either. I had no idea who did it and my landlord did not want to fix anything for our safety so my daughter and I packed up and moved in with my assistant.

My assistant was so gracious to take us in until I could get my head on straight but I still had the belief that every queen needs her own castle. We didn't stay long, though it felt like forever.

I had attained another home that had burglar bars and the works on it so I felt safe again. We had to put in a lot of work because it was a fixer upper, but my daughter and I did it.

Once that storm was over, I was laid off my regular job, the church I was attending folded. I swear I felt like life would never give me a break. I was still dealing with a lot of unresolved issues in reference to my personal life and now it had even leaked over into my church life.

It was the holidays when I had gotten laid off my job and I guess I could have taken it better had I done something wrong, but it was just a downsizing situation and there was nothing that I could do.

From that tragedy JGM Educational Consultants was born. I worked from home for a season and I had continued doing ministry gigs in connection with the book.

I was having a lot of trust issues at the time, the church had folded, I had lost my job, I was touring and the Lord made me put myself out there and reveal myself in reference to my past sexuality. The Pastors I knew had betrayed me, the friends I had left me. It was just way too much going on. That's when I got the assignment from the Lord to write my second book in 7 days.

I really didn't think I could do it or that it could be done period. God gave me strict instruction to write out all of the pain and hurt that I had experienced and close those chapters. This is exactly what I did. That's when I met "the Pastor."

I took this as a sign that I had to clear all of that other emotional clutter out so that I just knew that this was going to be the best relationship ever. He seemed to have his stuff together and so did I. We were both believers and seemed to be equally yoked, so I just knew this match was made in heaven for sure.

We dated for a season and everything seemed to be working out great. No one in the church knew we were dating because we never said it, but I am sure that they knew. He and I would share our schedules via email and would try to align them to find time for each other. There were very few issues in number, but the issues that we had were weighty. I questioned his sexuality and his commitment because there were a number of women after him, and he seemed to be entertaining it versus keeping them in their place. I had begun to pray about the matter and all things concerning he and I. Little did I know how the answer would come.

Divine Revelation

In my opinion, and statistics backs up my claim that homosexuality and drugs are the two hardest issues to overcome and be delivered from. One thinks that being with the same sex would be easier because you are so much alike. No one knows a woman better than another woman. I can only assume that the same holds true for a man, I don't know. On the flip side of the coin, no one knows better how to hurt someone than someone of the same sex as well. My struggle may not be the struggle of others, but I own it as my own. Some people's issues run deeper than sexual orientation; it can be their sexual identity. It is my desire that this chapter would become a conversation starter and even an educational piece for those who have misconceptions of the homosexual community.

19

UPSIDE DOWN-PLANE CRASH

Chapter Foreword by (my brother)

I remember when you told me that you were dating the pastor. I felt he was using you for the gift that God gave you. His church was growing because of your anointing. I came to help you out with the kids while you traveled and one day I got some really bad feelings. You later came and told me how he broke your heart and then to make matters worse the day you were about to fly out of town you, didn't make the flight and the plane that you were supposed to be on crashes and you lost friends and colleagues.

Chapter Foreword by "The Musician"

I remember like it was yesterday when Lolo walked into the church after hearing about the plane crash of her staff. I could tell something was wrong. She was normally able to come and ignite the service, but this day was different. She stood there and said nothing. When she finally found the strength to speak and told the congregation what happened, I just wanted to grab, hold and comfort her. As much as I wanted to do that, I also didn't want to ruin all that she had going on by allowing people to associate us together, especially when we weren't together at the time.

After finding out that she was seeing the Pastor, and witnessing how he neglected her in her time of need, I just wanted her to choose me, because I thought that I was the one who was going to fulfill her happiness and I was confident that we could move on and have a happily ever after. Every time she told me of his neglect, I wanted so bad to ask her, "Why not just pick me?" After a while I found the courage to do so.

I hate that our relationship didn't work but nevertheless, she pulled so much out of me and showed me so many things in reference to people, especially church people. Traveling with her, I saw the good, the bad and the ugly as it relates to the behaviors of the "saints." I still carry these lessons with me today and use what she taught me about discerning people and how to deal with them when God shows me who they really are.

I have known Lolo for many years. Over the years I have known her to be a courageous, loyal, on point, and a blessed individual. My biggest perception of her is her radical prophetic gift. My greatest moment of concern for her was when we found out that she had cancer because it was like a meltdown moment for her. Through it all though I knew without a doubt that she was greater than the disease and that she would surely beat it. I was most proud of her when the grandbaby came because, though I didn't know why, I saw a clear reconnection between her and God.

Little did I know that he would be her motivation to fight through the adversity of her cancer as well as our breakup. When I see, hear and think of Lolo I get excited because I know that she is a phenomenal person. Despite all that we have been through, I have always trusted her, her vision and her anointing.

The Journey Continues...

◆◇◆◇◆◇◆

I felt I was the closest that you could get to a first lady without being married and getting the official title. He and I shared our schedules, we prayed together, we ministered together, and we supported each other at his church and others. I knew his kids and he knew mine. I had been to his place and vice versa, but most importantly we were sleeping together as well.

I thought we were really on our way somewhere, and then I prayed that God would show me the truth, but I never said how I wanted it revealed. I was traveling a lot and I was really making strides in my personal ministry and solo career. I had my clothing line, I was ministering, I was modeling, I was a little bit of everywhere doing everything and I felt that life couldn't get any better.

I had a full team who did all of the hard work for me from the bookings to the financials. I even had a friend with his own plane that allowed me to use his plane so that I could ensure that I was home every Sunday and Wednesday to support "my man" and the ministry. Everything was going great except the fact that I was working myself to death.

The day came when I was supposed to head back out of town for a conference and I also had to go and see some mockups for my new clothing line. I also had to go pick up some financials as well and close out some other projects. I was headed to go and get that done, but I got a lot of pushback from family and friends. My brother was the first one to say no, even though he couldn't tell me why, but this was unlike him to say anything like that. I was also instructed not to go by my love interest. He saw how tired I was an urged me not to go and to just get some rest. Other confirmations came from my doctor, and even the pilot. Finally,

I accepted the challenge to stay home and rest and to even sleep through Sunday School and just go to morning service.

When I was on my way to church service that was when I got the call. It was the brother of the pilot who told me that the plane had crashed. All I could do was screaming and holler. I pulled over to the side of the road and I believe I said every curse word that was ever invented. I was completely numb. Why did God show all these people and not me? How could he take my friends and not me? How do I tell these families? What will I say? Five of the closest people to me in my business, all gone at the same time, and without me. So many questions, and yet no answers.

The first person that I called was the Pastor and I told him what happened. He went on to tell me about a dream that he had that he and I was riding in his car down this path and a plane went up into smoke.

Then I called my brother and he told me to come home because he was having some really bad feelings all night. I didn't know what to do. I was numb. I was speechless. I felt as though I couldn't breathe. I could feel my baby hairs rumbling through the breeze of my agony. Words cannot describe how I felt.

When I got to church, the Pastor was still not there yet and he told me to go ahead and start service. Are you serious? Do you not remember what I just told you? Are we just doing business as usual now? My life has been turned upside down in an instant! How dare you! I got there and just sat in my car with tears bursting violently from my eyes. I couldn't even think straight. I couldn't find a scripture. I felt completely useless and numb. I walked up to the pulpit and looked at the audience. I tried to tell my lips to part, but they wouldn't move. I tried to lift my hands, but they felt like a ton of bricks. Just to stand there took all I had.

Finally, I opened my mouth and told the congregation what had just happened and then I looked in the corner of my eye and saw the Pastor crying while looking at me. Right about then was when my legs gave out and I just remember the mothers of the church and the musician running to my rescue and praying for me. The Pastor just stood on the sideline. I felt so vulnerable and alone, more now than ever before.

The musician, "The Musician", had offered to drive me home but I declined. I just wanted to be left alone. I had a lot to figure out. I got into my truck and I left. I didn't care about nothing or no one, but my team.

I could see their families, their children, their spouses, all of them were minus a loved one and I felt like it was because of me. I blamed myself for everything.

When I got home my phone starts ringing off the hook. Family called. Friends called. Ministry colleagues called. None of my friend's families called. When I pulled myself together enough, I began to call them and what I got from them hurt worse than the initial shock of losing the staff. I found out that the families blamed me as well.

All five of the families had denied me the ability to attend the funerals of their loved ones, because after all I was supposed to be on the plane as well. If only they knew how bad I wished I was on the plane.

My phones wouldn't stop ringing but the interesting thing is that not one time was it the Pastor. The members called and Facebooked me. The one consistent person that was there for me the entire time was the musician, "The Musician". What she was doing for me was what I wished the Pastor would have done.

She stayed with me through the legal battles with the families, she held me through the denials of access to the arrangements, even though I personally paid for every funeral with money recovered from the projects that they helped me to book. That year was the first year that JGM was upside down.

A prominent Pastor mediated between myself and the families to allow me to attend the services of my friends. He told them of the hard time that I was having and how I needed closure just like they did. After much prayer and a lot of mediation I was allowed to attend the services. To this day the families will still not talk to me and will not allow me to publicize the fatalities of the crash, nor any of its details.

The only closure that I have of this time is knowing that I did the right thing. The fact of knowing that it just wasn't my time is my only resolution and way of making sense of it all. It also let me see the Pastor for who he truly was.

The relationship ended and for the longest, I blamed myself because I just couldn't shake myself loose from the tragedy that I just experienced. Not only that, I was also bothered at the fact that he was never there throughout the entire ordeal. Not to mention that he went on shortly to marry another woman whom he had been seeing at the same time he was seeing me. Just another devastation that I was not prepared to deal with.

Through it all though, the musician, was there and she soon became my lover, best friend, business partner and also one of my biggest life lessons.

Divine Revelation

I learned through this chapter that when we ask God for something, we have no control of how he answers that prayer. Through the sagas of this chapter, I learned about life, business, friendship, loyalty and loss but through it all, though my life felt upside down just like the plan landed, God turned it around for me.

20

ABUSE AND ABNORMAL
USE- "THE MUSICIAN"

You can't sing! They are better than you! You're no fun!

Abuse and **Misuse**

Your kids ain't shit! They need to go! All you need is me!

Chapter Foreword by Lolo's Life Coach

Abuse is not normal. There is nothing in the rule books that says it is and when you become involved in a controlling relationship, things can become physical, degrading, humiliating and a dark place from which you feel there is no rescue. That is far from the truth and it all begins with you changing you.

When Lolo was in such a relationship, she text me, called me and emailed me many times for advice and an opinion. She got both during the worst time and due to the manipulation she was under, it turned verbally abusive to me from both Lolo and her partner. That is how much control someone can force on to another person.

When you call for help, you have to be willing to break the chains that bind you and set yourself free. Free from intimidation, physicality, mental abuse, verbal abuse and financial abuse to say the least. One must be to the point of breaking to get the strength you need through God and family and friends.

As the person reaches out, you have to have the patience of Job to see it through with the person calling for help. It is not an easy journey, but it is obtainable.

Your strength and faith combined with that of others to create one large shield for the abused person can and will give the door an opening to create an opportunity to be released from abuse.

Lolo went through it all and saw that what we were all saying was the truth and after a very hard struggle, she emerged stronger and returned to those who love and care for her. She mended bridges and began to heal and regain the Lolo she used to be. It took tons of prayers and believing that God was the intervention and salvation needed from this part of her life. She fought through the obstacles and came out a winner. Just one battle in several she would face. Faith, hope, trust and perseverance for achieving what is right pays off.

Abuse is not normal or natural. There is always something that causes someone to be that way to another person but YOU CAN walk away and out of it before it is too late to do so. Reach out for help. Reach out for God. Reach out for a new and better you if you have been abused. You don't have to live this way and Lolo proves that.

The Journey Continues...

I was so unsure of how to write this chapter because there was so much that happened. In all actuality, I really honestly avoided this chapter because it was so painful.

Finally one night the Lord woke me up out of my sleep and told me to look up the 8 attributes of abusive relationships, define them and write the occurrences that happened within that attribute. It was still painful, but lessens my ability to become a victim of it again by having to relive it. I underlined the parts that I experienced in each definition as I retold my experiences.

1. Intensity

Someone you just met exhibits the following behavior: <u>LYING or exaggerating</u>; INSISTING you move in/get married/have kids immediately; <u>trying to win over friends and family</u>; OVER THE TOP gestures like expensive gifts/dates, extreme love letters; <u>sweeping you off your feet</u>; <u>BOMABARDING you with texts</u> and emails; behaving obsessively and non-stop calls.

When "The Musician" and I were together, we were intense, from our love making to our business ventures. We were committed to everything. We started off working together to improve churches across the world and to turn their music ministries around. We felt it would be easier for both of us if she moved in with me. My brother and both of my children were living with me at the time as well. My brother was there to help me with my kids as I traveled and I was helping him rebuild after an ended relationship.

In the beginning "The Musician" was winning over family and friends through our business ventures together. To others they just saw me and my "business partner" doing "business."

For the longest time I continued in that lie because I was too afraid to come out. In all of the abusive relationships that I was in, I never really came out and coming out was never an issue because they understood my world and the perception of the people in that world.

I was already in a very fragile state at the time of "The Musician" and I meeting, after the plane crash, so just her presence was intense enough for me, especially since the man that I was with was ignoring me and all that I was going through. "The Musician" would call and text me all hours of the day and night and at the time I saw nothing wrong with it because in the moment, that was what I needed. This is how she swept me off of my feet.

Now in hindsight, I can clearly see why it is important not to make any life decisions when you are in such a vulnerable place after such tragedy because clearly the costs can and will be great.

2. Jealousy

**Behaving IRRATIONALLY** when you get a promotion, job or new friend, **becoming ANGRY when you speak to the opposite sex**, persistently ACCUSING you of cheating, **resenting your time with friends, family, coworkers and activities**, DEMANDING to know private details of your life.

I already had all of my degrees in place at the time of meeting "The Musician", I was completing my coursework for my educational doctorates and fully encompassed in my dissertation. No one and I do mean no one, understands that anguish unless they have personally been through it. "The Musician" did the best she could to understand and even help me when she could. This was what I considered our bonding time away from work.

One thing that I have to say was that the music arena, as far our projects were concerned, was never really an issue. She provided the tracks and I wrote the music, we went in the studio and recorded and whala, magic happened. When we were in churches, she played and I sang and we instructed together, sometimes agreeing and sometimes not, but no matter what at the end, it would all work out beautifully.

We had become so close and nearly inseparable that when it came time for us to part ways and operate in our personal endeavors, we would get mad at each other. She would be angry if I didn't go to her gigs with her and I would get angry when she didn't understand that I had homework to do. I thought I had come up with the perfect solution and I would take my laptop to the night clubs with me so that I could experience the best of both worlds, I was supporting her and getting my own stuff done. We would always celebrate the completion of a class or an endeavor of mine with drinks and or a celebration at a gig.

It wasn't long before I found out that "The Musician" was doing more than drinking. She was also using illegal drugs. I never knew because I had never been with anyone who had this type of issue. I found out when I started seeing cut up straws laying all over the place, especially in her vehicle. The first time I found it, it was in her vehicle. I saw some white stuff and a straw and I asked her what it was. It's probably hard to believe that I didn't know, but you have to remember I have church smarts and book smarts, but I never really learned street life, because I was never in it. When I confronted her about it, she told me that the drugs were the way that she paid the musicians for our projects. I was floored!

I had so many more questions, I just didn't know what to ask first and I surely didn't know what to ask when it came to all of this drug stuff. Because of this I never asked about it, I just came to a point where I didn't trust her.

I had no clue as to why she was doing all of this, nor how long it had been going on. If I didn't know those things, I definitely didn't know how to help her. This made me question every encounter with her. When she was happy, I was wondering was she high, and when she was sad I was wondering was she feenin. Nevertheless in whatever state she was in, I knew that I loved her and I was going to help her through this because she was helping me through my grief.

"The Musician" is a multi-talented musical force. She can play a number of instruments. One of the first things that I noticed about her was one Sunday in church the head musicians were running late and we were still to start service on time. She started off on the organ. When the organist came, she jumped on the drums. When the drummer came, she took her regular place which was to play bass. When the sound system acted up, of course, you know they called on "The Musician" to come and assist with that. Never in my life had I seen a woman so versatile and being a music lover myself, she became my dream come true.

While she was doing her things well, there were a number of things that I had succeeded in as well. At the time of meeting "The Musician", I had my own clothing line, music career, preaching, prophesying, writing and of course my education. This became attractive to her. She would always call me with spiritual questions and I would answer them directly and honestly, more importantly I would give her scripture to back up my claims. Something that our Pastor at the time was unable to always do.

It seems like things would have went well because we were both so established in our own rights. Not true! It created more of an issue. I became jealous of her life and freedom to party and she became jealous of my ability to operate spiritually. Tough combination!

Now in hindsight, now I see that we were both standing in a place of silent jealousy and could not articulate it at the time because it was a reality that neither of us acknowledged or confronted.

3. Control

TELLING you how to dress, when to speak and what to think, showing up UNINVITED to your home, school or job, CHECKING your cell phone, emails, Facebook, going through your belongings, timing/ FOLLOWING you, monitoring spending/WITHHOLDING money, sexually coercing you.

It wasn't long before we began to try and control each other to a certain extent. I was accustomed to dressing a certain way in my area of expertise and she was used to dressing a certain way in hers. I remember I would go to night clubs with heels on and things of that nature and that was not always appropriate attire for the venues in which she played.

Every time we would go places, my "downloads" would begin.

Download is what we called it when God began to speak to me about a matter or a person. "The Musician", and anyone else who knows me for that matter, can always tell when it's happening. Sometimes it became overwhelming for me which was often the times when I would decline to go with her to a gig; she would then be upset and question my decision.

To keep confusion down, I would just give in and go. When we would get in the car, I would tell her all about the people that we saw and I would share with her all of their business, even though I didn't know them. This gift became fascinating to "The Musician". This was a world that she was not used to, and she was operating in a world that I was not used to so both of our fascinations became addictive.

It wasn't long before "The Musician" would tell me how to dress when I go to her gigs which was tennis shoes and jeans and a t-shirt, all of which I barely owned, but I changed the way that I dressed so that I wouldn't stand out like a sore thumb. She became more selective of the people that she introduced me to, especially when it came to the man who supplied her with her drug product.

For the longest time, I didn't know who he was and then the night came that he came to a gig. "The Musician" took off running towards his truck. Seeing her running, of course, I ran after her. I saw the whole thing. She gave him money and he gave her product. They hugged as if they were old friends to play it off; after all we were in public. This was the day that changed a lot of things; I knew then that her issue was far from over. I questioned her about it all and of course she denied it and tried to make me think that I was crazy.

I was normally the one who took care of all of the financials, after all I was the primary breadwinner of the house and she would just give me what she made from her gigs as a supplement. That night was no different, except the fact that I had the money that she got paid that night, so my question was, "Where did she get the money from?" Another layer of trust was broken that night.

When I realized that she was still struggling with this habit, I began to ask about all of her money. When she went to a gig I wanted to know how much she was making, I paid all of the band members out of that and I kept tabs on what was left. However, on her regular job, I was not as informed. Her paychecks were direct deposited and I had to trust her to give me the money or to pay the bill that I had assigned to her that week. I wasn't sure what she made and what was left. I can only assume that is where her habit money came from.

As time went on, I got tired of asking about it all and trying to keep tabs of everything and I just got to the point that I damn near didn't care no more. I felt that this was her demon to fight not mine, but I also knew that if she was to ask about my distrust and insecurities with her that I would assure her that her addiction and behaviors were the root.

Now in hindsight, I know that I should have left when I first discovered the drug use and the lies, but I didn't. Love will make you do some funny things. It wasn't like it was all bad, so I chose to ignore the bold prints of issues and the underlying manifestations and I stayed anyway.

4. Isolation

INSISTING you only spend time with them, making you emotionally, psychologically or financially DEPENDENT, preventing you from seeing your friends, family, or children, FORBIDDING you from going anywhere or speaking to anyone, keeping you home.

When "The Musician" moved in with me, my brother and my two children were there in the house with me as well, and I had two dogs that we all loved dearly. We had both of them since they were born and they were very much a part of the family. My brother was staying there with me to help me with my kids since I was traveling so much and he had just moved down and was trying to find a job and all. My daughter was in college and my son was finishing high school and so of course my agenda stayed full and I couldn't do it all alone.

When "The Musician" came along, all eyebrows had went up because I hadn't been with a woman in years. Rather than confronting me with their concerns, my family just sort of went along with it and trusted my decision. Some days I really wish they would have challenged me on it. Nevertheless, most of my time was dedicated to accompanying "The Musician" at her gigs, while we were still doing our collaborated musical stuff as well, and I was still in school, I was also still very much involved with my own career and personal endeavors.

After a while "The Musician" felt that it was time for me to stand on my own two feet. She consistently exclaimed that my kids and my brother needed to get out on their own.

My brother had finally found a job. He was using my vehicle to get back and forth to work, my daughter was using my vehicle to get back and forth to college and to work, my son was walking to and from school so he wasn't really an issue and then of course "The Musician" would use my vehicle for gigs even though she had her own van.

When my brother got his first paycheck, he spent his whole check on getting a car and he didn't contribute anything to the household and due to my recent tragedies and me paying for five funerals, my finances were a wreck. I got fed up and told him that he had to go. (Little did I know that would wreck our relationship for the longest time.)

My son was finishing high school and my daughter was in college and I knew I had to start preparing for the empty nest though I never wanted to face that moment. I tried to explain to her the relationship that I had with my kids and to help her see how crucial they were in my life. I wanted to be to them what no one was to me; present, loyal and supportive. We went round and round about this and finally I gave in.

I thought that I had a master plan that made me stick to my commitment to them and to her as well as a way to thrust me into the new life I was itching to embrace. I told my kids that I was moving. I was over half done with doctoral school and I was ready to finally start my career as an educator and my present location was not where I wanted to reside anymore, but I also wanted to make sure that they were okay as well.

I told them that we were going to move out of the house together. I would get a small apartment for "The Musician" and I and that they could move into their own apartment. I promised that I would stick around in my apartment for one year to ensure that they were okay and stable before I moved on and that is what I did.

"The Musician" and I had moved into a small two bedroom apartment. One room was the bedroom and the other was my closet/office. The kids lived a little over a block away in a small one bedroom just until my son finished high school and then he was going to move into an apartment on his own. That was the plan that would launch all of our independence.

My daughter had gotten "The Musician" a job where she was working at and they were working together though we all lived separate. This was where the feuding between them started. I can only imagine how my daughter felt seeing "The Musician's behaviors at work and knowing that "The Musician" and I were together, yet she was displaying behaviors that could be perceived as though she was single or open to infidelity.

"The Musician" had this bad habit of hanging out after hours with coworkers, and most of the time I was not invited. I was working so I was often too busy anyway but it came to a point that the invitations began to stop which took away the option to even attend. There were a number of occasions where I wouldn't even know where she was. Oftentimes I would find myself begging "The Musician" to spend time with me and she would always holler about how busy she was and how many hours she had to work, she even began to exclude me from her gigs.

Now that my kids were gone and on their own, my brother was gone and no longer speaking to me, all I had left was my little dog and as much as I loved her, she wasn't much company. To top it all off, my lover was appearing to be loving on another.

Though I had no proof of it physically happening, I did notice "The Musician" talking about this girl to me all the time. They were always on the phone together and had even hung out a few times, but probably more than I knew, naturally I became suspicious.

I will never forget my last residency that I had to do for school; I had to go to Phoenix. I was so tied on what to do. I knew I had to go to finish school, but I didn't want to risk losing what I thought to be the love of my life either. I didn't want to make her infidelity easy, but I had no choice, I had to go.

While I was away, I was so obsessed with the idea that she was cheating on me that I began to check phone records and saw the same number popping up time after time again, even though she promised me she wouldn't talk to this girl anymore and how she was going to be home missing me so much. I knew it was the girl's number because I had called her.

When I confronted "The Musician" about it, of course she lied and said she hadn't talked to the girl and then she pulled the, "it was work related" card. How could this be when the calls were at odd hours in the morning and all hours of the night? I'm sure I don't need to say how much this affected my studies in Phoenix. I had even considered having an affair while I was there with some random dude who was trying to talk to me, but of course I didn't do it.

When I returned, that was when I had told "The Musician" that I was leaving. I couldn't take the torment of thinking of her being with someone else while I was making sure she didn't need or want for anything, in any manner. This was my first attempt to leave. Of course, then she turned up the romance, the sex, and most of all her presence in my life. Her actions placed a band aid on the issue for a moment.

Now in hindsight, I can see how unhealthy this relationship was and how "The Musician" was trying to have the best of both worlds. She had a real stable woman at home who made sure that all business was squared away, all bills paid and all needs were being met. On the other hand, there was this young, cute, skinny irresponsible girl who fulfilled the fun stuff and had some of the same issues that "The Musician" did. I should have left then, but I didn't.

5. Criticism

Calling you overweight, UGLY, STUPID, or crazy, ridiculing your beliefs, ambitions or friends, claiming, they're the only one who really cares about you, making you feel bad about yourself, BRAINWASHING you to feel worthless, accusing you of being a bad parent.

As I applied pressures and threats of me leaving, that is when the criticism began. I would try to convince her of why she needed to be faithful and change her ways if she wanted to keep me, and she was busy trying to tell me all of the things that I needed to do to "make me better." It was always I needed to lighten up and stop being so "Jesusfied", I needed to lose weight, I needed to stop this and start that and I would take note of everything that she said because above all I wanted to make things work because in my heart and mind, I really did love her.

First step, weight loss. I felt as though I couldn't do it on my own because of my schedule and my lifestyle as far as my travels and stuff and eating on the go so I looked into something that would give me head start into the weight loss. I needed something that would remind me of my commitment, even when I didn't want to be committed. I began the process of the Lapband surgery. Going through all of the counseling and trainings and even the pre-surgery diet was intense, but "The Musician" was there through the whole saga.

The day of the surgery came and my brother and both children were there. I was pretty heavily medicated so of course I don't remember much except the fact that "The Musician" was so super protective of me that day. She treated me as if nothing and no one else in the world mattered that day. If only I could have this treatment for a lifetime, life would be grand.

It was an outpatient day surgery and there were no complications, so I was allowed to go home hours after the surgery. "The Musician" took a day or two off to stay with me at home and to make sure I was okay and the kids were in and out all the time. "The Musician" didn't even want to go back to work when it was time to return. She would make my soups and drinks that I needed with the times that I needed them. She placed it all in the refrigerator with the times I was supposed to eat and drink certain things. She did the same things for my meds and she would call and wake me up to make sure that I stayed on my schedule. If I didn't answer she was on her way to check on me or wake me up because most times I was too medicated to hear the phone.

In the midst of all of this we were also preparing to move to Dallas to start our new life together. It had been a year now. My son had graduated, my daughter seemed to be doing great and was stable, and she was even preparing to finish college. Our biggest preparation though was the fact that my daughter broke the news to me that she was pregnant. "The Musician" and I both wanted to find this dude and beat him to a pulp, but it was consensual and he didn't do it alone, so we just both had to accept it.

Now in hindsight, I can see the manifestations of the criticism. Even if she never said it, seeing her actions, flirting with skinny girls, to changing the dynamic of who I was "Jesusfied" as she called it. She even made me feel that she was the only one who really cared about me especially with my seizure condition coming back into play. Yes she was often the one there to help me through the seizures, but the truth of the matter is that she was also a big cause of the seizures as well.

6. Sabotage

Making you MISS work or school by starting a fight or having a MELTDOWN, <u>being needy when you're busy or doing well</u>, <u>making you believe your crazy, alone or helpless</u>, HIDING your money, keys or phone, stealing your belongings, <u>DESTROYING your self-esteem.</u>

When we moved to Dallas, I just knew it was a new beginning for us. Though half of me didn't want her to go, I also didn't want to be alone in a new city either. I wanted to show my commitment and undying love for her so it was at this time that I came out to the world that I was gay. I made this a major part of my life at the time. She had even proposed and we were planning a wedding. I thought the roughest part of our relationship was over. It seemed we both had what we wanted, each other.

My kids were grown and gone, and her son had always lived with his grandparents and would only visit us occasionally. We were in a new city, neither of us really knew anyone, nor did we know our way around so we were stuck together like glue.

My coming out made me lose contracts, ministry associations and affiliations and a whole lot of other stuff, but none of that mattered to me as long as I had "The Musician". I knew that she had my back, or at least I thought I did.

We had begun looking for a church home. Specifically, we wanted to be a part of a gay church so that our sexuality did not have to be hidden but would be accepted and celebrated. We also wanted to befriend other "healthy couples." I, for one, needed new associations because I was still exploring this lifestyle that I had never really openly operated in and I needed to know how that was done.

Finally, we found a church and we thought that we were on our way. It was a gay church that was predominantly African American. Everyone seemed so cool and loving and we even found some other gay couples to hang out with. It really seemed like things were coming together and then the seizures reared their ugly heads again.

My epileptic condition reoccurred nearly at the onset of my relationship with "The Musician". I had seizures before, but never this frequent and it had even gotten to the point that they were trying to put a timeline on my life because of the seizures, saying that it was affecting my brain causing it to deteriorate in some way. Nothing was helping me, not the meds, not the exercises; none of it, the doctor just kept urging me to limit my stress.

It was coming to a point that going to church and seeing all that I was seeing was becoming a bit overwhelming to me. I saw a man who identified gay, who was married to a woman that was a stud (male identified gay woman). I saw a man who was transgendered into a woman who had an identical twin who was straight. It was just so much that I couldn't wrap my head around it all and it became overwhelming to me. I soooo wanted to figure it out and understand it all, but there was no way that I could especially because none of it aligned with what I had already been taught or had researched.

I told "The Musician" one particular night that I didn't want to go to church, but she insisted. I went and the whole time I was there, I kept feeling some kind of way. Finally, I told "The Musician" that I had to leave because I was about to have a seizure and she tried to help me out but I collapsed before we could get out and I had a full seizure right there in the back of the church. I am not sure what all happened, as I lose memory when I am seizing and I become unaware of what was happening. All I know is that when I woke up the next morning at home in bed, "The Musician" was in her feeling and had made this long post on Facebook about the occurrences of the night and how I was treated.

I tried so hard to make sense of it all but nothing would come back to me. I tried talking to her but she was all upset and in her feelings, I wanted to reach out to the Pastors and church members but they were in their feelings as well. I tried to bridge the gap between all parties but nothing would help and now that "The Musician" had made this a public service announcement on Facebook and fans began attacking the church and the church was trying to defend themselves.

Needless to say, no good thing came from that and the relationships were severed. For the longest, I had so many questions but no one to answer them. I do remember that we did have a meeting but from what I saw, it was too far gone and too much damage was done to try to salvage the relationship.

Now not only was I excommunicated from the straight churches for being gay, now I felt ostracized from the gay churches for some reason I didn't know due to this occurrence. By this time, now "The Musician" has a job and is back to her old ways of hanging out with friends after work again and again I am at home alone.

I was in the process of planning our wedding, doing my dissertation, working, and planning a baby shower for my daughter who was now near delivery and having complications with her weight and all. All in all, just more stress, which of course lead to more seizures.

Finally I broke down and told "The Musician" that we were going to have to hold off on the wedding planning especially since the wedding was not until March and it was only September and that I was going to focus on one thing at a time to keep my stress down. I had to put things in order as they were due. First was my dissertation (now), the baby shower (October), the holidays which was November and December and then the arrival of the grandbaby in January then all of my attention would be on the wedding. She said she agreed and that my plan was fine.

Not sure what she meant when she agreed, but she made things a lot less than fine for me. The fights occurred more and more, she became more distant, she was hanging out with work friends again (new city, same stuff) and finally it happened, she cheated.

Now in hindsight, I can see yet another opportunity for me to break free. As I write these occurrences, I know that I have a choice to see it as a blessing or a curse, I can be the victim or the victor and I choose victory. I knew that her actions were not my fault.

7. Blame

Making you feel GUILTY and responsible for their aggressive or DESTRUCTIVE behavior, blaming the world or you for their PROBLEMS, threatening SUICIDE/self-harm because of something

***that you did/you want to leave, always saying, "This is your FAULT"
or "You made me do this."***

When "The Musician" cheated on me with a coworker, she tried to make it my fault by saying that I was too busy for her, I was no fun, she was bored, she felt left out and all of the other classic avoidance excuses that are given as a redemption or justification for the actions of cheaters. Now I may have been naïve about a lot of things but this one thing I knew for sure. Lolo was doing her part.

When I finally woke up and said, "Enough is enough, I'm done!" Then that was when the pimple was popped. She probably said sorry more than my grandson calls my name on any given day, and that's at least a thousand times. However, I'm sorry wasn't good enough. This was now our third location and third big relationship blow.

In our first place, I found the drugs and I let her come between my family and I. In our second location which was our apartment, where it was just the two of us, she was having some sort of emotional, if not physical affair with her coworker and now this. No more, I can't, I won't, I don't have to and I didn't!

Now in hindsight, I see this as the rebirthing of myself. I had finally done it. I had broken free from the cycle of her abuse. This declaration of freedom was not just about her but also it was my freedom from family, churches, religion, children, and even my own expectations. I was free now!

Though we were still under the same roof things were never the same and I wanted to keep it that way. Lolo (the kind loving Christian) had finally met Lolo (the street fighter who had been locked up in a mental institute). They became acquainted, but also became allies and had agreed that they would work together to get me out of this fix I found myself in. Yes, there were days when Lolo had to pray and Lolo had to cuss and because they were both coming at "The Musician", and at times she didn't know which way was up and who or what she was dealing with, but finally my liberation became my top priority.

8. Anger

<u>OVERREACTING to small problems, frequently losing control, violent <u>OUTBURSTS</u>, having severe mood swings, drinking or partying when upset</u>, THREATENING to hurt you or loved ones, <u>picking FIGHTS</u>, having a history of violent behavior and making you feel AFRAID</u>.

"The Musician" always had an angry disposition and was very "gangsta" which was part of my attraction to her honestly, but the problem was she had never met the gangsta in me. No, I had never been to jail, never had any legal issues, but I would always tell her that the difference between she and I was that she got caught and I didn't. After my declaration of my decision to leave her, naturally, she went through a plethora of emotions, the grief and the anger.

For months we went through the vicious cycle of abuse. We "honeymooned" where she would apologize or try to make up for what she did, and then she would blame me or just ignore or deny the abuse. Then we experienced the "tension phase" where everyone in the house was walking on eggshells, there would be threats and intimidation, fear, guilt or just outright unpredictable behavior on both ends. Finally, we go to the last phase of the cycle which was the "violent phase" where, the abuse actually occurs, violent behaviors arose and we were back to the place of the emotional, and or financial originated.

This went on from at least November to December and then the anticipation of the arrival of the baby took over everyone's focus. His birth literally saved my life.

Divine Revelation

Have you ever been through something that shook you to your core? Have you ever felt that life had dealt you a hand that you knew you couldn't play because you were not taught how to adequately play the game, but you knew that it was too expensive to forfeit? That is the experience that this chapter speaks of. It tells of how I found myself in an abusive place and

how I finally found the strength to take my life back and move
forward, but of course it was not without consequences.
For years I had been in relationship after relationship, I
thought I had seen it all. I felt like my kids needed a father
and that the presence of a mate made me a better mother
and so for years I would get in relationships where I would
do everything that I could to make people love me.
I bought them, took care of them, sexed them, I cooked, cleaned
and nurtured them to the point where I catered to issues that were
not my doing. I "fixed" them at the expense of breaking myself.
In addition to this I would also try to be mother of the year for
my children. Teacher of the year for my students, employee of
the century for my employers...all in all I wasn't okay with just
existing, I had to supersede existence and step into excellence at
all costs. The costs often wind up being myself and my sanity.

21

SEASON OF SEPARATION SOLIDIFIED- MOVED TO MY NEW CITY

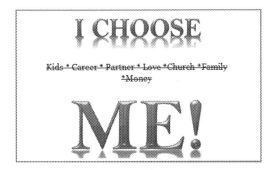

Chapter Foreword by Close confidant

I met Lolo during her encounter with cancer as well as when she was making the transition/decision to end her relationship with her partner at the time. It has been over three years to date that I have known Lolo and I have come to know her as a tenacious survivor who perseveres even when giving up is an option. My perception of her is that though she is serious and educated, she is also driven by her passion; she still has a witty side that attracts and captivates the attention of others.

During her season of separation, I would say that she did okay. Did she dot every "I" and cross every "t"? No, but who of us would have been able to, given all that was on her plate at the time. At moments I saw her falling apart, I saw her confidence low, but most of all I saw her fearful within the confines of her intelligence. She battled with the fear and anxiety of not only her health, but also the demise of her relationship. She was viciously seeking answers to live, even though her relationship was dying.

What I love about Lolo is her ability to share openly with the world the fluidity of her sexuality and the struggles that come with it, but more so her ability to change the thinking of her counterparts in academia as well as religiosity and continue to make people ponder on their own beliefs.

I believe that this book is going to take people out of survival mode and into vision which is produced by actions outside of their comfort zone. Lolo is an evolving piece of work and I am proud to know her and to call her one of my spiritual daughters. Keep on doing what you're doing daughter and as you move forward, don't forget to reach back and pull someone else along.

Lolo's Close Confidant

The Journey Continues...

During this tumultuous time in my life, I was clinging on to every inch of life and hope that I had. The day finally came when I said enough is enough. I can't take it anymore; the hurt, the pain, the persecution, the abuse, the mistreatment, the lies, the slander, and the abandonment. It's not who I am and I'm worth so much more. I called everyone into the living room and I made the announcement, "When my lease is up, I am leaving and I am going alone!' Little did I know that this statement would create days of chaos in my life that I would never think that I was strong enough to get through.

Today was the day that I changed it all. Today was the day that I said, enough is enough. Today was the day that I told myself that I was good enough and that I was okay just the way that I was. As much as I love my grandchild, I realized I was too far spent to be effective as a grandmother, as much as I loved my children I realized that the years of self-neglect had now caught up with me. As much as I tried to love my mate and make a difference in her life, I realized that we are all grown and the fixing of her issues was not my assignment any longer. So I took a stand and made the declaration that this is it!

I always knew the weight of words but during this season I got the revelation. When I declared that this is it and I am done with living beyond the expectations of people and trying to prove a point that no one took notice of, heaven and earth heard that declaration and acted accordingly. The problem is it seemed that hell took it personal and acted with a vengeance.

It was not like this was an overnight aha moment, it was a progression of events and personal revelations that led to the building of my strength to take this action. So I guess the heat was just building. That heat led to me experience infidelity in my relationship, my daughter risking her life having a baby, my son losing his job, me experiencing health issues that would only escalate after this declaration but nevertheless, I said it and it's done so now I must face the consequences of my words. A test of my faith, the testament of my commitment to God and me, is what it was all about

After I made my declaration I couldn't even look at the faces of everyone because I know my heart would have melted and I would have given in so I said my peace and I left the room. Everyone sat there as though they wondered what just happened, but no one really said a word. It was the most liberating, but also the most tantalizing thing that I had ever done for myself. I knew what it felt like to be betrayed and abandoned because I had been there before in my life when my mother died and left me alone to raise my daughter alone, nevertheless, I made it through and it made me the responsible woman that I am today.

I kept telling myself, "Stick with it! Stick with it! Don't look back! Don't change!"

This meant that not only am I making them move but I have to move as well and I had made no provisions, I had nothing up my sleeve, this was a clear faith walk. I went against everything that I knew to do like pray first, wait for a response, make a plan, make a list of pros and cons and all of that stuff that I would normally do before I make a life decision like this but this one, I heard the voice of the Lord and I expedited his command.

I knew that I hated the school district where I was and I didn't want to be there anymore because I couldn't play into the politics and foolery that I witnessed on a day to day basis. First plan of action FIND A JOB!

Work

I knew that I was well educated and had the credentials to do anything that I wanted, but I love to teach because I am a believer in education and I love children. So I set out and started applying at various districts. I also knew that I hated the city I lived in because the people were not friendly and I didn't know much about the place but I also knew that I didn't want to be around this city getting out of the toxic relationship that I was in because there would be no peace. With that people kept telling me that they knew people and that they could get me jobs here and there, but I wanted to be where God wanted me and I knew that he would make sure that I was at peace and happy. I had a friend who said that she would help me find a place in my new city and something in me just kept saying, "No, that's not the plan!" I called one day and asked her had she even been looking and she said, hesitantly, "Well I mean…." I knew then I was on my own.

I had applied at the local Independent School District and had gotten an email that I was approved for the teacher's pool. I didn't know what the next step to take was so I did nothing. Finally one night, the Holy Ghost said create an email and send it to the schools that you are interested in and that is what I did. Within 24 hours, I started getting email responses. I had applied at so many districts and at so many school following leads and the like and finally one day, I got a call and the principal and I stayed on the phone my entire lunch break. We laughed and bonded as though we had known each other for years and without even laying eyes on me she hired me.

Though it was a miracle I still didn't give up looking, after all I didn't have a contract in my hand so I started scheduling other interviews. I told her what I was doing and she said she understood, but she also knew that this was a divine setup and that God would intervene and that is what he did.

It was all logistical as to why she couldn't give me a contract at that moment and as a result I continued my search. I had a Saturday full of interviews scheduled and I was on my way down to my new city when I got the email that had my contract attached. Now, to find a place to live.

Home life

I knew that I was going to be living alone but there was a manner of life that I had become accustomed to and I didn't want to go below that standard of living so I took that Saturday that I had scheduled interviews, emailed all of the schools that I had appointments with to let them know that I wouldn't be there and I took the opportunity to go and meet my principal and see my new campus. After spending the day with her, I started looking for an apartment but I kept hitting dead ends, either it was the neighborhood or some other reason why I couldn't move into them. So I came home a little down hearted because I felt as though I did not accomplish much on my trip.

I went to work that Monday and I received an email from an apartment complex that I never seen and don't even remember inquiring about but it was in my perfect price range with all the fixings that I wanted. I made plans to make another trip down to see the apartment and to take care of all of that business and I took my daughter with me. When I went to see the apartments, I have to admit that I was not impressed so much so that I started not to take it and then she showed me the location of my apartment. PERFECT! The other apartments had no view; they faced the back of a shopping center. My apartment faced green pastures with a walking track and a playground. The other apartments had parking under the awning but it was far from their apartments, and my parking was right by my apartment door which would make all things convenient for me. I knew this was it.

I told my daughter that I was not taking any of my old furniture as in my bed and the living and dining room set and that I would give those things to her and buy me more and sure enough on this trip, I found new furniture at an unbelievable price and they would even hold it until I moved.

With all of these things in place surely I thought the rest of the transition would be easy and that is when all hell began. My health began to fail.

Divine Revelation

I saw these occurrences as the beginning of my metamorphosis into the next season of my life. Though I was unsure of how it would all turn out and how it would all come into play, I still stuck with my declaration and my commitment to God and told him that no matter what through this, as with everything else, I trusted him, I just didn't realize how much those words would mean.

22

---·◆◆◆◆◆·---

THE GREAT SET UP-CANCER

Chapter Foreword by Lolo's Life Coach

Battling cancer is not an easy thing. I should know. I have battled cancer for over 30 years. Not much I haven't been through in doing so.

I was a natural place for Lolo to come to for advice and a heartfelt ear to listen. Lolo was terrified at the term "CANCER" as it had taken friends and family from her over the years and you wouldn't be human if it didn't have some sort of effect on you. You think the worst from the get go when you are told. You don't hear the words of good outcome from the doctor; your mind is focused on only one thing: the word that kills more people every day than car accidents. When Lolo first called me and asked how I made it through cancer, I told her that I had to go deep into faith and use that to pull myself up and tell myself that I have too many things to do to let this take me on its terms. I told Lolo that she had to focus on prayer and that she too is a mother, daughter, and sister and she has to be the strong one for them. She had to fight with everything she had to show her family she had the strength and commitment to come out a winner and beat cancer no matter what the course of treatment and she was determined to win on her terms.

It was a tough fight and needless to say, she came out swinging and a champion. She turned it over to God and He handed her the victory. Now I fight renal failure, sepsis of the blood and a spot in my lungs but I stand firm that you can be survivor or allow yourself to succumb. I choose to survive. I am a victor and not a victim. Lolo and I both are winners. It's a God thing to be a victor and survive.

Chapter Foreword by (my brother)

One day I was going about my daily routine and I get the phone call that no one ever wants to get. My sister had been diagnosed with cancer and given a few months to live. God and I had a serious talk.

I told him, "God you have taken my mom, my marriage, my child, and now you are trying to take the only real love I have, my only reason to keep living? I will not let you do this to me! What have I done so bad that you feel the need to take away everybody that loves me?" But she fought and I prayed and the world prayed and she made it through.

My sister and "the musician" had moved to another part of Texas than where I was. She had been working with "the musician" and that relationship blossomed into a marriage proposal. She asked me how I felt about it. I told her that for some reason you seem to be happier with a woman than you are with a man. Then she started making wedding plans and life was good so I thought.

Later she tells me how "The Musician" had been cheating on her and hurting her. I tell her to have her removed off the property and soon she tells me she was moving back to my city where it all started.

She moved back here and she encountered some challenges with the job market and still being used for her gifts. But no matter what comes her way, she always overcomes the obstacle.

The Journey Continues...

Not only were the seizures more frequent but I was having these pains in my stomach. I thought that it was simply stress so I ignored it. My living environment had become unbearable. I felt like I couldn't do anything right. In the winter, I had postponed our wedding because I was clearly doing too much. I was working on my dissertation, working, my daughter was having complications with her pregnancy, I was trying to plan her baby shower, and I was trying to plan our wedding and trying to hold my relationship together.

I was trying to prioritize my life and segment it in a bearable way for me especially because I didn't have any help with any of it. So I made the best decision possible by postponing the wedding planning so that I could take each thing as they came. I had turned in my dissertation. The wedding was not until April anyways, so I chose to focus on the baby shower and ensuring that my daughter was okay. All hell broke loose.

I was accused of putting my daughter first as usual. I couldn't understand this because I did what I thought any good mother would do, except the one that I was with because after all her child lived with her parents. I never had that option. My kids have been the only real consistency I had in my life, so yes they do come first. Due to her displeasure with this plan, she was late for the shower and did all she could to ruin it. Then for Thanksgiving I did our norm, which was to go to my family's, and she chose not to go and that is when she cheated on me. Not only did she cheat on me but she made my trip hell, so much so I came home early.

When I got home my spirit let me know that something was not right about the situation, but we all know that God has a way of revealing things, even what we don't want to see.

It was late at night and she had fallen asleep early. I was fast asleep and the Lord woke me up because I kept hearing her phone going on off. She didn't move and I knew that her parents were ill so I immediately started praying that all was well.

I went to her side of the bed after unsuccessfully trying to wake her. I couldn't find her phone so I went back to bed. Then it started ringing again and again. I tried to wake her. I am assuming she was high, but I had no proof except the fact that she was sleeping so hard. I laid there and the Lord said, "Follow the charger cord." I did just that and found the phone nestled away under the bed next to the night stand. I got the phone and saw a number of text messages. It had a males name as the contact. The messages read, "Is that the bed that I tore your pussy up on?" My heart dropped because the sheets looked like mine. I looked further into the text messages and saw that this had been going on for some time.

Immediately I woke her up, by any means necessary. I pulled the covers off of her and shook her vigorously until she woke up. I immediately told her that she had to go be with the man she was sleeping with. My heart was racing, my head was pounding, and my hands were sweating. I was completely discombobulated by the whole saga because I never wanted to think that this could happen to us.

She immediately tried to calm me down and explain but there was nothing that she wanted to say that I wanted to hear. "I'm sorry" was unacceptable! "It's not what you think" sounded like an insult. "Let me explain" infuriated me, so her best bet was just to be quiet and leave peaceably. Of course it didn't happen that way.

The lies started rolling out like the red carpet at the Oscar awards. The only truth she told was that it was a woman and not a man. Then it was, "We are just friends." Then it was, "We only kissed." I made her call the girl and tell her that she was engaged and to make a decision.

I asked her if she had oral sex with the girl and she said "No"…Lie! I asked her if she fingered the girl, and she said "No"…Lie. The girl told me everything. I even found out that the girl had rode in my car and they had went to a gig together while I was home sick. While on this outing, "The Musician" told the girl that she was paying all the bills and taking care of me, and we all know that wasn't true. I couldn't make heads or tails of it all and why I had to be treated this way. All I knew was that I wanted her gone. I took her phone which was in my name and anything else that she had of mine that I was paying for and I declared I was done. She had no place to stay and nowhere to go because the girl told her that she didn't want anything to do with her anymore.

"The musician" called her mom and told her her side of the story and of course her mom believed her and said that it was all my fault and she told her I was crazy. I could care less! After all this, I went full force into preparing for my grandbaby. My daughter was finishing college in a few weeks and was coming to stay with me so that I could be there for the birth and assist her with the baby.

When my daughter got there, matters escalated, as to be expected. "The musician" became so jealous of my daughter and the attention that she was getting from me that she would stay out even more and even longer. She was doing all she could to make things right with me, but I was too far removed from the relationship.

As time drew closer to the birth she too was getting excited. Finally, the time came my daughter went into labor. I refused to leave her side as any mother should. She was experiencing the same complications that I had with her. Her placenta was breaking. They wind up having to do an emergency C-section. I was a nervous wreck, but excited all at once. My personal life, for once, was not even in the back of my mind. I was focused on one thing and one thing only and that was to see my grandbaby and make sure that my baby was okay.

"It's a boy!!!"

After staying at the hospital the entire week we (my daughter, grandbaby and I) all went home. I was excited beyond belief. Naturally my daughter was on bed rest and I had to go back to work. Both "the musician" and I had left our numbers for emergency purposes. "The musician" was closer, and I was over 30 minutes away. I couldn't get home fast enough each day.

When my daughter was finally able to go back to work, "the musician" got her a job where she worked, just like my daughter had done for her in days gone by. Big Mistake! At first, all was well. My daughter worked at night and I was working during the day, so we swapped out caring for the baby until he got old enough to go to daycare.

When he was finally able to go to daycare, we found one right near my job. I would take the baby to and from daycare because my daughter was clearly exhausted after working all night, even though I was clearly exhausted from working days and then staying up at night with baby. "The musician" would help sometimes, but I tried to keep that to a minimum to keep confusion down. However, there was still confusion because "the musician" started complaining about me watching the baby. I didn't really pay her any mind, even if I agreed. I saw my daughter doing the best she could and I wanted to honor her effort by giving her a hand.

This went on for a while and then all of a sudden, I started not feeling well. I was fatigued all the time. The pains in my stomach were getting more intense. I began bleeding with every bowel movement. I thought it was just me getting tired from my daily routine and then I thought my hemorrhoids were just flaring up, but the bleeding became more intense. I kept trying to figure it out and self-medicate until one day it felt like I was in labor and no matter how much I went to the bathroom, it still kept feeling like I had to go again.

I didn't tell anyone because I didn't want to worry my daughter and I didn't feel like hearing "The Musician's mouth. I knew that in some way she was going to make it my daughter's fault. I took off work a little early and I went to the doctor and he immediately ran some tests. I had no idea what he was looking for. He seemed as if he knew instantly what it was. Nevertheless, after a battery of tests, the doctor reported to me that I had cancer.

My knees buckled, my heart sank, my eyes watered, but it seemed as though the tears were afraid to fall down my face. So many questions came to mind but I didn't know which to ask first, so I said nothing. I left the hospital and went straight to Prayer Mountain.

Prayer Mountain is a beautiful place in Dallas, overlooking the city, where people go to pray and worship and even fellowship. I would go there often to get a break from the craziness that was in my household. "The Musician" hated my daughter and the feeling was truly mutual. There is where I told God all of my displeasures with my life, and yes even with him.

I felt like I was pretty decent individual. I had a great heart, had told everyone that I could about him. I made myself transparent, even when it meant public ridicule and shame and even ostracism. I had endured all that the enemy had thrown my way, so I wasn't sure why I had to go through this now. I told him, there are so many ways that you can take me and there were so many times, why choose this way. I think this is the day that my relationship with Christ was consummated on a deeper level. I knew that I had no one but him, and that no one but him could help me.

When you pray sincerely, it's not all about you talking and walking away, you have to sit still and hear him speak so that is what I did. After hours of me crying out to him and actually falling asleep there on Prayer Mountain, I heard him so clearly say to me to get three different opinions and not to tell one doctor about the opinion of the other. That is what I did.

In two weeks' time, I went to two different doctors and attained other opinions. I did not tell the doctors about each other I just told them of my symptoms and let them all run their tests. What I didn't know is that each time you let someone open you up; you cause the cancer to become stronger and even spread.

When I went to doctor #1, he told me that I had cancer in the early stages that was really nonstageable and hard to detect, but very much present and defined. When I went to doctor #2 he ran his tests and he told me I was a stage one which meant now it was developed, but localized only to my colon. By the time I got to doctor #3, I was at a stage 2, which meant that it was still localized only to the colon, but was become more developed and headed to the more serious stages.

I went back to doctor #1 and I told him what I had done and he really ripped me a new one. I had done nothing that he said, I had missed all of my counseling appointments including the dietician, and for that my cancer had become more aggressive not to mention that the additional colonoscopies exposed my site which made it grow.

I was very transparent about my feelings about the whole process. I told him that, speaking as the patient, being told first of all that you have cancer is enough for one day, but to add insult to injury to be inundated with statistics and numbers and probabilities and prior cases and treatment options and diet changes all in one day was wayyyyyy too much for someone like me, especially seeing as no one in my family had ever had the disease, so my only experience with it was holding the hands of friends who had it. I also went on to tell him that as a new patient, I was ignorant to the terms that he was using and I needed real world examples of what I am looking at and what does all these stages mean.

I thank God for my doctor because he was amazing after that moment. He still ripped into me for what I had done but he knew my heart was in the right place. I wasn't trying to hurt myself. He understood and took me step by step and did my cancer education sessions himself. He explained it in a way that now I felt confident enough to tell my family about it. I didn't tell everyone just my children, my best friend, my dad, my brother and my mentors. I felt like this was fragile information and I didn't want everyone praying for or on me so I urged my family not to tell the world because I wasn't ready for that.

I remember when I told my family and all of their reactions. My best friend lost it for a moment, but quickly came back as she always does, and gave me encouraging words. My mentor immediately went into prayer, my brother screamed, cried and hung up, my dad went silent and my children were both no good to anyone, not even themselves. I remember when I told "The Musician", she seemed unbothered, but I had no time to focus on that, I had to make me a priority now.

As we began talking treatment options, I was adamant about working and finishing the school year especially since there were only weeks left of school. He told me that postponing my treatments could have some serious consequences. We did the first two cycles of treatment until school was out. We did immunotherapy and targeted therapy which was some very strong and expensive pills and creams to keep the cancer localized and well behaved. This made me super tired, loss of appetite, I had rashes all over and my attitude became worst. The pain meds took care of the pain for the most part.

I was taking over 11 pills three times a day plus using the cream. I hid my prescriptions from "The Musician" because I was not sure what her next vindictive move would be. I told her what she needed to know as she needed to know it which was not really much and not really often because she was never home anyways.

The cancer had become a bit more aggressive, but was still localized so my doctor started me on a series of chemo pills in addition to the meds that I was already taking. He knew the possible side effects of the chemo and he also knew how adamant I was about working so we came to a compromise for the pills. To take a normal dosage for one week and then he doubled the dosage for the Memorial Day weekend which was a time when I didn't have to work. I had never been so sick and weak in my life.

My children both came to my rescue that weekend and they all took turns caring for me. "The Musician" was in and out because she had gigs scheduled. My daughter took the day shift with me; my son took the night shift watching me and the baby. I was so out of it that weekend that I can barely remember it, but I do remember the fact that my children took care of me that weekend which felt like repayment of all the years of my struggle with them. They were miraculous. I was so super tired and fatigued. I was nauseated, I couldn't keep anything down. They had to set alarms for my med times because the times were stagnated. There were so many meds that I couldn't keep one of the cute boxes, we had to use zip lock bags and write the times on them to keep it all together. It wasn't easy, but we made it through.

Then the night came when it all came to a head. I remember "The Musician" and I were lying in bed asleep and I felt the worst pain ever. It was like my water had broken, and I was ready to push. I had no idea what was happening to me. I just knew that it hurt and the only thing that I could liken it to was childbirth. What do women do when they are in labor? Breathe! I remember breathing like I was taking the last few breaths before pushing the baby out. Breathing in and out and in and out and in an out. "The Musician" finally woke up and asked, "What's wrong with you?"

"I don't know, it just hurts. Something popped and it hurts like hell!" I replied.

Then she said words that will ring in my spirit for the rest of my life,

"Well can you breathe the other way because your breath stinks?!!?" "The Musician" said!

Those words knocked the wind out of me. My legs wouldn't work right so I just rolled out of bed on to the floor and crawled to the bathroom in the most excruciating pain I have ever known and I sat by the bathtub.

That night I had prayed like it was no one's business. I prayed as though no one else in the world existed but me and God. I told him as I sat there with tears in my eyes and blood all over the floor that this place (my bathroom) was my destination in life. I was caught between my past ("The Musician") and my future (my grandson) "The Musician" was in the room to my right, my grandson was in the room to my left and I was in the adjoining bathroom that connected the two rooms with blood all over the floor and pain I couldn't explain. Here was my prayer:

"Lord, look, I don't know what you are doing, but I believe that your hand is in all of this. I have had some struggles in my life, but none compares to the one that I am in right now. I am begging you to help me out of this, heal me, deliver me, and restore me. I am not talking about money nor material things; I am talking about restore me back to you. Take the taste (desire) for this woman and this lifestyle from me and let me be free again. Free to love you and free to worship. Free to be happy and free to be whole. First thing though is to please take this pain away. Allow your blood to cover my blood loss, and let it mean something spiritual, because it was the power of your blood that heals me in every way and it will be the power of your blood to make me whole. Please God!"

I wish I could say that it was immediately that the pain and the bleeding stopped, but as I laid there in the puddle of blood, not knowing where it was coming from and why it was coming that I cried like never before. I wept from the deepest place of my soul and my spirit. I had prayed before, but as simple as this prayer was it came from a different place.

While crying, weeping and praying in my heavenly language, as I began to continuously call his name because no other words made sense to me. I noticed the pain had stopped. I didn't feel the gush of blood when I coughed. I felt a small ounce of strength but nothing that I felt that I could get up and do anything with.

Now since the pain was gone, I asked God to strengthen me to get up and clean this mess up before my daughter comes home. I didn't want to be the one to explain to her the occurrences of the night because I had no words and I don't like to sound stupid. God honored my request.

I got up and took a shower, cleaned the bathroom and went and laid in the bed with my grandbaby until it was time to get up and go to work. When I dropped the grandbaby off to work, I called my doctor and I went to straight to his office.

A week had passed since I took the strongest doses of my chemo and now I was back to the regular doses. My dreads were dry and brittle and I was losing them piece by piece. To this day they are still uneven and I leave them that way intentionally.

I get to the doctor and as I get out the car a loc fell to the ground. I got to the door and the wind blew and I lost another one. Finally, I make it to the door of the doctor's office and he takes me straight back. I recall for him the occurrences of the night. He looks at me with tears in his eyes and said, "Lolo, you are not alone in this! Do you know that you could have died right there in the floor? Do you realize that you could have bled to death? Why didn't you call 911, hell, why didn't you call me?

His words became blah, blah to me. All I wanted to know was am I okay? I think he could tell that I was not with him because he stopped with the lecture and began his imaging tests. He looked around and around. It was so painful because he was poking and prodding and looking so hard. He took the scope out and then ran blood. Then he did a stool test. Through all of these tests he wasn't saying anything and I was so weak and fatigued, I just let him do whatever.

Finally, he and a team of doctors came in and all looking at me as though they had seen a ghost. I was fearful, I didn't know if I was dead or dying, but I just knew that something wasn't right, even though I felt good besides the normal weakness.

The doctors asked me to recall what had happened the night before. I took the last inch of strength I had to tell them. One of them said, "Wow, God!" The other walked away in tears.

"Can you all just tell me something? Damn enough already?" I screamed!

Finally my doctor came to my bedside and said, "Lolo look at these images. This was three weeks ago and this is today."

I looked at the images and I noticed they were different but I still didn't understand what I was looking at.

He went on and pointed out the cancer and said "before chemo…. after chemo". Everyone was so excited, but I was still lost. Finally he said, "It is almost all gone!"

I ran the whole battery of tests again because I couldn't believe my eyes. I did the imaging and see nothing but a small superficial spot. I ran your blood and it is near normal. I looked in your stool and explored that and I see small traces. He told me that he didn't want to continue the aggressive measures because it was attacking my good cells and they wanted to build the good cells back up, not kill them off.

He told me that the plan of action was to take me off chemo for a week and schedule my appointment in my new city which is where I was moving to in the next week or so.

I couldn't wait to get back to work and tell all of my coworkers that had been praying for and with me as well as tell my family and friends. I thought that the worst part was over and in my mind; I thought I was on the road to recovery. Not only was my health seemingly better, but I was getting ready to leave and start my new life.

"The Musician" had moved out by this time and life was seeming to get a little easier and less stressful. Away I moved and my new life began.

Divine Revelation

I titled this chapter "The Great Set Up" because I chose to see my cancer as a set up and my treatments as purification. I think that the illness served as a launching pad for the new life I was about to begin. I learned so much through my cancer encounter. I learned things such as who my real friends are, how much my family loves me, and that my relationship with Christ was and is vital. Most importantly, I learned that when you are in a crisis such as that, you learn what is most important involving Christ. It wasn't about what I wear, where I sit in church, whether it's a man or a woman who speaks into my life and all of the other frivolous matters that Christians fight over. All that mattered to me is that I had direct access to the throne and that God heard my cry and answered in his own way and time. This is where the journey back to me really began.

23

DATING DISTRACTION-
COMPULSIVE DATING

Chapter Foreword by my cancer caretaker

I came to know Lolo when she moved back to the city in 2015. Though she started off as a pain in the butt, I came to know the deeply spiritual and intellectual woman that she is.

My greatest time of concern for her was when she was going through her chemo and radiation because I witnessed the pain that she was in, the sickness that she felt as well as her physical weakness that came as a result. Seeing her travel through that season with such grace made me tag her as one of God's many blessings.

I was there for the duration of her battle with cancer. I feel like I had the privilege of meeting her at a time when she was the most difficult and I have now come to appreciate the woman and the survivor that she is today.

When I met Lolo she was in so much pain, not just physically from the cancer, but mentally from the torment of the uncertainty that comes with the illness. I did all I could to help her through her insecurities and abandonment issues.

Lolo was looking for wholeness for all of her broken pieces. She wanted someone that would help her through her pain and sickness. I didn't see her dating as a distraction, but more so as a quest to find someone who could and would step up to the plate and love her despite her current situation.

I couldn't help her with her physical pain, but I did all I could to help her emotionally. The combination of the physical pain she was in, the mental anguish that she was dealing with the uncertainty of her health and ending of her past relationship with someone who walked out on her during this storm, and then of course the medication was a lot for anyone to handle. Her mood swings would lead me to make sure that I had on the whole armor of God before I even knocked on the door. I got all of the side effects from all of her issues, especially the trauma that was her cancer, but I still loved her despite it all.

I was so proud when we got the word that her cancer was in remission. Our new quest was to get her to functioning normally and when she got to the point we both grew in our faith that God can and he will.

The Journey Continues...

After moving back to the city I was in a state of bewilderment. There was so much going on in my life at the time that I didn't know which way was up. It was the first time ever that I had lived alone. For the first time I didn't have to consult with anyone nor think about what they liked or wanted. For my entire life, I lived with my brother and mom and then exchanged them for my kids and my mate. I was always having to be responsible and be the model citizen and now it was my turn to finally do me, whatever that meant.

The only issue with my new "free" life is that I was bound with cancer that was only being progressive in its attacks. When I got to the city, the spot was still there and still the same size so they decided to start the next round of treatment which was radiation. They did that for two weeks. I was assigned to doctors that were to start my treatments immediately upon my arrival. Due to my severe nosocomephobia, or phobia of hospitals, that manifests in a dangerous blood pressure increase I was enabled by insurance to have a home health professional to assist me. During that time I was looking for anything and/or anyone to distract me from the many issues that I was dealing with.

I was battered and torn because it was literally too much going on at one time. I was dealing with the cancer, the medication, the pain, that abandonment of "The Musician", the infidelity within our relationship, the leaving of my children, and of course the care of my grandson. It was summer time, and naturally I was not at work so I just needed something. I wasn't sure as to which way I wanted to go even though I told God I was done with women. I stayed to myself for a week or two and then I met my cancer caretaker.

She was the first person that I met off of a dating site. She was so everything to me. I was afraid to tell her about my sickness because I thought that she would run away like "The Musician" did. However, I couldn't hold it for long as the treatments were beginning to take their toll on me. My hair was becoming more brittle and I was losing locs. I was constantly tired and I could barely keep any food down. I finally told her what was going on with me and to my surprise she accepted it. We started off as friends and it wasn't long before it led to more.

At times I really felt like I was losing my mind because as much as I wanted to be alone, there were times when I couldn't be home alone and I would have to go to my cancer caretaker's house and stay. She always made me feel right at home. She would cook and clean and do anything that I asked her to do. Who could ask for more? Me, apparently!

My cancer caretaker had started working long hours and sometimes that pain was too intense, so I would get back on the dating site to find others to entertain me and distract me from my current situation. That's when I met someone else. I told her too about my situation and she too was very supportive. The only issue is now I was having feelings of guilt on top of everything else that I was going through.

I was remorseful because I had made God a promise that I wouldn't date anymore women. However, in this time I needed the tenderness of a woman and not the strong arm of a man. I now had two women that would do any and everything for me and I appreciated it more than I could articulate. I was never without one of them by my side. The problem was all of my feelings were involved with both women. I knew I needed them both, there was no way around that truth, but I could not choose between the two. My fix was to push them both away. The next dilemma was they both loved me back and knew what I had been through and vowed not to do the same thing "The Musician" did.

One would take me anytime I wanted to see my kids and the other would always take me to Wal-Mart, which I hated, and tried to make me walk to build my strength back up. In fact the only fight that and I had was about me using the handicapped cart at Wal-Mart.

I would always fight with her and tell her that there were handicapped people who needed that cart and she would always say, "Yeah, you!" Every time, I would take offense to that, and pout because I didn't have the strength to argue and walk away.

Everything was great with my cancer caretaker and I until one day she took me to my best friend's house to see my grandson and she sat across the room and was looking at naked women. How disrespectful was that? The worst part was she showed the pictures that she was looking at to my brother in law. The funny thing about the relationship that he and I have is we may not always get along, but definitely go to bat for each other.

Though he didn't say anything to her, all we had to do was look at each other and we knew what was up. I was so offended; I immediately had my cancer caretaker take me home. We argued the whole way home, and I knew that wasn't good for me health wise, but I was so hurt and I needed her to know that, especially seeing as she had knew what I had been through.

Now I was down to one lady and she was great as well until she provoked a flashback. By this time both women knew about each other. I had just gotten the news that my cancer was in remission and I was ready to turn up, as much as my feeble body would allow.

I couldn't have sex for a while during treatments so she and I decided to celebrate in that way. I told her I wanted it rough and, as usual, she aimed to please. We both got caught up in the moment and the pain had gotten so intense. I kept telling her to stop, but in the moment she didn't hear me. Before we knew it, there was blood everywhere and my body was wreaked with pain. I had to tell her that the encounter reminded me of the time that I was raped and the pain reminded me of my cancer.

When I told her about how it made me feel, we both shut down and cried. It took me a while to get over that incident, but I was so angry and in my feelings about my cancer caretaker and "The Musician" and now her that I let my anger overtake me and I ended it with her.

I tried getting with another woman a few weeks later but she scammed me for the little I had left and while I sobbed over that situation, God reminded me of our deal and my promise. I had completely forgotten. I think I felt that if I didn't honor my word to him, he would bring my cancer back. Need I say I never touched another woman again? I answered that call to repentance and I never looked back, but it didn't stop my dating shenanigans.

After that I went on a dating frenzy. I had no one to hold me accountable and slowly but surely I was getting better. My weight was filling in right and at all the right places, and my broken locs, were trimmed to look layered. I felt like every word of Fantasia's song, "I'm Doing Me!"

Day after day, night after night, it was never a dull moment. I was really living life out loud and on purpose, and then it all came to a screeching halt with one phone call.

Divine Revelation

This part of my journey was the most liberated that I had ever felt. Being able to date freely was fun, but exhausting. I didn't realize just how much I WAS NOT missing. I realize now that it was only God's grace that kept me safe through this season and I am forever grateful.

24

✦✦✦✦✦✦

THE GREAT REUNION-MY
DAUGHTER COMES HOME

Chapter Foreword by My daughter

I honestly don't know how to feel about the cancer. I was scared and disappointed. Scared because I would be losing my best friend and I thought it was the second round of a generational curse except my baby had just been born. I felt disappointed in my mom because I had told her the reasons behind her stress seizures was due to "The Musician" and because she didn't remove herself from the situation with her then God was giving her one more chance to leave.

I was disappointed in myself because out of everything that I could have done I had a baby. What a way to add stress!!!! What a way to be a support system!!! I was letting myself have it that last trimester because "The Musician" was letting my mother have it with all of the verbal abuse because of just my presence. Then after I had my baby even more stress came. I just felt like more of a burden, but I didn't know what to do.

I was trying to stand up for myself and my mother, be respectful so I didn't cause any more problems, hide my anger and depression to make sure I didn't stress my mom out more and give ammo to "The Musician". I didn't know what to do or say. It was like we all had guns, but had each other's bullets instead of our own so what was the point in having the gun.

LOLO

Then when mommy finally got the strength to leave, and she insisted on taking my baby. I let her. At the time I got it, but afterwards I felt responsible for her remaining sick because instead of her resting, getting treatment, and getting better she was running behind my child making sure he was okay..... more stress.

Now looking at it from where we are now he was her strength. When I came home it was both of us coming into our healing process. What a great reunion!!! We're all together and helping each other like always.

The Journey Continues...

When my daughter called and told me that everything on her job had went through, I had mixed feelings. She had gotten her transfer to the city, she bought out of her lease, and she and her boyfriend were coming to take care of "my grandbaby".

I guess they were coming to take care of me as well, even though I didn't think I needed to be taken care of. However, I knew I would not be wilding out like I was before with them there, because they held me to a higher moral standard so back to the model citizen I went.

When my daughter got home, she immediately noticed the change in me. She noticed that before, I wouldn't dare go to bed with dishes in the sink, not even a glass, but now I would stack the dishwasher and keep it moving. She noticed that before I washed clothes nearly, if not, daily because I hated seeing dirty clothes in the house, now I washed clothes maybe twice a week.

Life for me drastically changed when I was inflicted with cancer and even when I became an empty nester. Things like that, which were crucial to me once upon a time, weren't so crucial anymore. I just wanted to live in freedom and peace.

I didn't realize the curse of my mother's excessive cleanliness bondage was gone. I realized houses were made to be seen and homes were made to be lived in and enjoyed. Now, I'm still a clean freak, just not obsessed by it.

When they came to the city, the deal was they would be with me for a year. They needed time for her to save money, for him to get a job, and for them to find a place. I have to be honest, I needed their help financially, because I had paid for all of my treatments and things out of pocket, whatever insurance didn't cover and I was trying to get back above water, but I didn't really want to be restricted on what I could and could not do in my own house because they were there.

Though I had known her boyfriend since they were in high school, I was not comfortable with him. As much as they talked about marriage and being together, I knew it would never happen, nevertheless, I went along with it all.

Finally it all came to a head, my ministry had begun to take off again and I was getting bookings from everywhere. Now I was definitely glad that they were there to help me, but the love fest was short lived.

The boyfriend couldn't keep up with the pace and his priorities of finding and job and helping with his "new family" so he ran.

Divine Revelation

This chapter reminds me of how, yet again; my daughter came to the rescue and saved me from myself. When she was born, she filled a void that I didn't even know existed and now, over twenty years later, she was doing it again. I think I can say with assurance that we are each other's best friend. Though I know we get on each other's nerves at times, we both know that there is no one else on earth like each other that will have our backs and give us the support that we give to each other.

25

DESTROYED-FALSE ENGAGEMENT AND HEARTBREAK

Chapter Foreword

Elizabeth and Mary were divinely connected in a manner that only God could orchestrate. There is a saying that people are in your life for one of three reasons; a reason, a season and a lifetime. The interesting part of the puzzle is figuring out why they are there and then handling them accordingly. Abandonment is one of the worst forms of abuse and the reason why is because many people abandon us without reason or at least they don't tell us what the reason is. Spouses may cheat and abandon the household, as the victimized spouse and even more so the children of the abandonment, they walk through life with a burning question that asks, "Why?" When we grasp the concept of the triad as to why people enter into our lives, we are able to alleviate those questions and continue on with life believing that though I may not know why they left or what the purpose of our encounter was, I know that it will be revealed by and by. Holding on to the question is a form of self-abuse because it creates the inability for us to move on and enjoy life knowing that our destiny is not tied to them but to the encounter in which we had. I definitely had to quickly grasp this concept, especially as a single woman who was in the dating scene. I would find myself heartbroken when I thought that this one was, "the one" only to find out he wasn't. What I learned is that with each date and each heartbreak, I became more equipped for the single life and I also became more keen to the games that people ran when their intentions were less than pure. Yes people come into our lives for a reason, season or a lifetime but what they all have in common is the fact that it is all about kingdom connections for the betterment of the individuals involved.

- 365 Revelatory Words for Any Given Day (2017)

The Journey Continues...

Now that the ministry was back in full swing, I was formulating a new team and trying to come up with a game plan of how to get my life back.

Normally for my birthday I take myself on a trip and have a little fun but this particular year, I couldn't because I was booked from here to there. I was excited to be back on the road again. For once, life after cancer seemed normal.

Two thousand and sixteen was a strange and difficult year for me. For my birthday celebration, I was in San Antonio on Thursday at a church I had never been to and I received a word that said,

"This year is going to be an extraordinary one for you! You have been praying for something and God is about to bring it to pass. It's not professionally either, it's personal."

I was a little bewildered because there was not just one thing that I had been praying for personally, that came to mind, but I just put it in my journal to pray about.

I was at a church on Friday and received a similar word. Saturday morning, my team and I were ministering at a prayer breakfast and received a similar, but more specific word. This one said all of the above, but she added,

"This year God is going to send you your husband, and you will be married before the end of the year!"

My mind was blown. I asked myself, "—How can this be, I'm not even dating anyone? Nevertheless Lord, your will be done."

That evening, I had to minister at another church in the city and received the exact same word I was really starting to get spooked, but I knew God was up to something, so I started to get excited.

LOLO

That Sunday I went to morning service at a church I was attending and one of the ladies who was a member there but followed my personal ministry as well asked me how I felt. I told her I was still trying to take it all in. Would you believe Sunday evening I go to another church and get the same exact word yet again? If I was to just tell this to anyone no one would believe me, but I had witnesses and they all rejoiced with me.

Now I began to walk in expectation. I didn't know how, when or who, but I had no choice but to believe. I had met some people on a dating site, yet very few marriage material in my eyes, but I kept hope alive. I met men who were single fathers looking for a baby mama. Not me! I met men who were looking to be taken care of. The devil do be lying! There were some who were looking for sexual aerobics, but I ain't that chick!

Six months had past and I saw the husband of the woman who mentioned marriage to me in her word. I saw him lurking around me, but I had no idea who he was. Finally, he came and said something to me. He introduced himself and asked me about my status, seeing as my hands were still bear. I assured him that everything was still the same; I was still very much single. Now I was talking to someone at the time, and I was hopeful, but nothing really came out of it.

A couple of months later a man that I had talked to earlier in the year had reappeared. He has apologized for the way things had went the first time and said he wanted to marry me.

There was no ring or formal proposal, but we talked about it every day. We started talking again in late August/early September. For some reason, I never really had a peace about the whole situation, but I was going with the flow because of this prophecy that I received and the fact that the year was nearing a close, I felt like this was my opportunity.

There were many things that made me uneasy. He only came to my house, I never went to his. He had met my children, his was living out of state, so I never got a chance to meet nor talk to them. These are just a few issues.

Now though there were some things that made me uneasy, there were also some things that made him believable. He shared his financial situation with me. He shared his work schedule with me, and we spent a lot of time together.

He talked about the wedding so much, I figured I better start making plans. Although I didn't want to have a wedding, he had never had one and I wanted to give him something that he never had.

I told my boss about it and that was when everything took a life of its own and quickly spiraled out of control, but in control on the other hand. When I told her, she immediately offered me to have it at the school, which used to be a church. One coworker has a band, and offered to play for us. Another couple of coworkers wanted to decorate, others wanted to do the food. When I tell you the wedding planning was nearly done within 48 hours, I mean just that.

I told him about what was happening and he began choking up. He finally started to come clean. He told me that he was already married and they had already filed for a divorce and that the sixty day waiting period would not be over until January 2017. Devastated to say the least, I had come too far to turn back now, so I accepted it.

He then became more distant, and I became more skeptical. I was trying to make myself excited about it all, but it just wasn't working. I had gotten to the point that I was losing sleep; my appetite was gone for food and for him. Instead of more confirmations concerning us, I had more questions.

In November, I got news that "the second woman" had passed away and I was devastated, especially seeing as I was supposed to go and visit her the same weekend of her funeral. I immediately told my significant other, calling him in tears and anguish. He was seemingly too busy to come see about me. This reaction was way too familiar and set off my inner alarm in a more prevalent way. Mind you, this is the second death I had experienced in less than six months and he wasn't there for either.

Filled with despair, I was ready to call off the relationship and wanted to talk to him in person about it all. All of a sudden, when I tell him I need to talk to him, he has a "family emergency" and his "mom gets sick." He called me frantic and despite my storm, I wanted to run and be with him. He wouldn't allow me to come, and he wouldn't answer the phone.

A day or so later, I hear from him and he tells me that all is a little better, so I make plans to see him that weekend because that was the first opening in my schedule. He agreed. Of course, when the time came, he had another "family emergency." This time he said his daughter was in an accident on the school bus and was rushed to the hospital so he had to run out of town to check on her. I offered to take off work to accompany him and again, he refused. I tried calling him the whole weekend. No success. I was worried sick. I kept calling and texting and praying. He told me it was bad before he "left" so I was left thinking the worst. I reached out to his family on Facebook to see if they could or would respond and I got no response.

Days later he came back and actually had the audacity to get upset with me for worrying and contacting his people on Facebook. I knew then that my spirit was right. I didn't need anything else to happen, no more confirmations, I was done. I called it off. I had never felt so dumb, naïve, and manipulated in my life.

I went to work the next day and asked some of the seasoned women, how did they know their spouses were the ones. They responded, "If you gotta question it, he ain't the one." That was all I needed to hear. I called, left a voicemail, and text him that it was over. He immediately began calling me back, but I wouldn't answer. I didn't want to hear another lie. I was over it.

After much begging, I finally agreed to meet with him. He kept on apologizing and kept reminding me, "It's not what you think!" This sounded so familiar and only made me angrier. He then went on to tell me that he and his wife were going to cancel the divorce and work it out. For some reason that didn't sit well with me, but frankly, by that time I didn't care.

I had done way, too much for this "relationship." I had changed my phone number as we had agreed, but he never did it. I had offered him a key to my apartment, and he didn't take it. I had accepted the proposal, without the ring he never bought. I purchased a phone because outside of the city, he supposedly got no signal. I wasted time, energy, and emotion. I felt completely destroyed by this whole saga.

I wish I could say that it was over already, but there is more. A few days later, in the middle of the night, my phone starts blowing up from Facebook messenger and my voicemail. I checked the messages and it was a woman. She was crying and I heard him in the background trying to plead his case to her. I was very reluctant about returning the call, but I did the next day.

I messaged her back on Facebook. She told me she was his girlfriend.

She asked how did I know him and I told her. I answered all her questions and she unknowingly answered all of mine. She sent pictures of the event that they were at together with his family the weekend of the "tragedy."

She told me that he told his family that I was a crazy stalker when I asked them about the said, "tragedy" on Facebook messenger. She went on to tell me how she had discovered that I was not the only woman he was talking to besides her. Apparently there was a plethora of others and she had contacted them all.

Immediately I went into ministry mode. I knew the hurt that she was experiencing all too well and I wanted her to know that she/we were worth much more than what he was dishing. She cried and cried on the phone and I could hear the brokenness in her spirit, and though I too was a victim of this foolishness, clearly I was not as invested as she was. She said that they had been together all year and I only had a few months. After hours of conversation and me being a listening ear and an encouraging presence, she still decided to stay with him and I wished her well.

After all was said and done, I was devastated and emotionally destroyed. I didn't know which way was up. How could someone as intelligent as me be so gullible and fall for all of the signs that I point out to others. It hurt, but not as bad as it would have had my spirit not gave me the emotional cushion that I needed to experience this blow. I knew that I had some personal work to do and only God could help me do it.

Divine Revelation

Deception happens to the best of us. For the longest time I beat myself up about this entire situation from the believing in the prophesies, to the falling for his game. I didn't understand how someone such as myself with such a discerning heart could fall prey to the lies that I had just encountered. I knew that I had some choices to make and that these choices could no longer be superficial, they had to be God led, so I knew what I had to do and I did it.

26

BACK TO ME-REDISCOVERING MY GOALS

Chapter Foreword by Lolo

Again, A Gain

There are times that we have been taught that it is negative to have to repeat a thing. I remember one time I was on a conference call and we were having testimony service, so to speak, and one lady kept saying I went through this and I went through that and I said, "Lord not again!" she said. My spirit was punctured by the word "again" and it changed the very element of my being. In that time God spoke to me and said, "Please let her know that to do a thing again is not bad as long as there is a gain.

As an educator I transferred this revelation not only to my life, but also to my classroom. I remind my students it's not always a matter of if you got it all right or all wrong, but the gain in knowledge that you make each time. So remember as long as your again comes with a gain rest assured God is pleased with your progress and you should be proud of yourself.

The Journey Continues...

The Devastation of the occurrences of my prior season sent me into a deep depression. In that depression, I was able to recognize that I had let my guard down in so many ways both spiritually and naturally. I know how to hear from God for myself. I know how to seek the face of God when I receive a prophecy. I also know how to adhere to my discernment and not override it though; free will allows me to do so.

I knew what I had to do to get back up again from this explosive situation. I had to turn my plate over and seek the face of God in the most intense way ever. I knew I had to encounter God in a more excellent.

When the new year of 2017 came I knew I wanted a different and better year. I wanted different for myself personally. I wanted God to do something super with my natural existence. I started going to this church down the street from my house, and the very first time that I went, God spoke directly to me through someone else's situation.

The preacher was talking to this young girl, even though we were both standing at the alter together.

He used the man of God to tell her that he (God) knew that she had contemplated suicide and that she was more depressed now than ever before. He went on to say how he had seen that she had given up on church, on God, on her gifts, on her talents, and on the ministries that were within her, but God said it was time to recover all.

I nearly hit the floor simply because everything that he was saying was for me. I had made up in my mind that I didn't want to hear from any other person telling them what God supposedly told them about my life. I wanted only to hear from God directly because all that I had went through in 2016 stemmed from the false words that I had received, and held on to and this man knew that. Clearly God had shown him and I was grateful.

I attended the church for a season, but I couldn't join. I had too much baggage and I needed to be healed first. The Pastor had been talking about a 40 day fast that the church was going to partake in during the month of February. I sought the Lord about joining the fast and that was when it all began. God told me that this year for my birthday I was going to start an individual fast as well as do the fast with the church. I was in awe, but I also questioned if I could do it. My spiritual and natural self-confidence had taken a hit this last year and I questioned myself about everything, and I do mean everything.

God kept speaking to me about this fast until my spirit got stirred up. I started my fast on the 18th of January though God had told me to start February 1st. I was walking in such expectation of what he was going to do in my life and what he was going to tell me. From the first day the instruction came pouring into my spirit.

One of the first things God reminded me of was my dream of writing a book every year for the rest of my life. In 2011, when I wrote my first book, I said that I wanted to write one book every year for the rest of my life. I did that and then life happened. I was working on my dissertation and battling all other types of issues which is what brings me to "The Journey Back to Me."

The kickoff of this journey is me catching up to my own personal goals and aspirations of catching up on my writing, thus the five books for the year of 2017.

When I got that instruction, I gasped for air. I am self-published, so my first concern was the financial obligation that this feat would take, but God said, "That ain't yo business!" I then thought about the time and the material, but God said, "That ain't yo business!" I had no idea what I was going to write about. Thank God for the fast giving me specific direction.

I was mortified because it wasn't like these were short books and I had no idea how in the world I was going to find to complete these works, but God said, "That ain't yo business!" I continued to seek his face for direction and he gave me the timelines. I was to complete the devotional first by March 1. Then do the interactive classroom book by April 1 and finally the data driven classroom by May 1. I was to put all of these on the publisher's desk by the end of April. May 1 I was supposed to start working on my personal memoir, The Journey Back to Me. I was to have that book done by the end of June and then the relationship book done by the end of July.

By the time the first three books were done and ready for release, I would be ready to put the last two books on the publisher's desk in August.

He further instructed me about the release of these projects. My mother died when she was 43 and I will be 43 in January of 2018 so in honor of her, I was to release these books on my 43rd birthday. My mother passed 5 months after her 43rd birthday and that would be when I launch "The Journey Back to Me" tour. I was still wondering how I was going to do all of this, but God said, "That ain't yo business!"

All of this was a part of the process to the journey back to me. In this process is where I rediscovered my passion and purpose for life. I had been working on the 365 devotional for years and I had even solicited others to help me write it in days gone by with no success, THIS TIME I was able to complete it on my own. The floodgates opened up and the revelations came forth and I completed the book ahead of schedule. The other two books were completed ahead of schedule as well and were done with ease.

The hiccup came when I hit this book. The hiccup was not with the timeline, but with the content. I had no idea how emotionally intensive this project would be, but I also had no idea how rewarding it would be as well.

Divine Revelation

This rediscovery did a lot for my self-confidence after so many blows in the years gone by. Getting emotionally involved in my own success again helped me in so many ways. More than that, being able to hear the voice of God so clearly also let me know that he and I were still good. He has provided the finances, the energy, the time, the resources and even the people to assist and hold me accountable and now I am back to me. My love for God, my passion for ministry, my commitment to my crafts were all reignited and it was a welcomed distraction from all that I had recently been through.

27

The Reconciliations of My Life and the Occurrences Therein

During this season of intense conversations with the Lord, there were several reconciliations that he revealed to me and had me to notate for the sake of closure.

From Life to Lifestyle

Definitions

- Life- the general or universal condition of human existence
- Lifestyle- the habits, attitudes, tastes, moral standards, economic level, etc. that together constitute the mode of living of an individual or group.

Reconciliation

There was a great level of freedom came when I realized that what happened in my life did not determine my lifestyle. Just because I grew up one way did not mean I had to remain that way. If you grow up in poverty does not mean that you have to remain in that impoverished state. You can be the chain breaker in your family that determines the way that your family may choose to live. This is the case for my family. My mother may have lied to me about her collegiate endeavors, but for me it was going to be

LOLO

a reality especially because she said I couldn't and wouldn't. I determined and purposed that I wanted more and better for me and my children and thus we have become.

Unfortunately many people, thanks to the media, have their priorities a little mixed up. Some look at people on TV and think that those people are living the life. What does this mean? The statement that they make or think implies that they have made a god out of material things. The detriment to this action is because if people see the items as "life" then that means by default, they believe the absence of these things means death.

I used to think that the presence of "things" was life so I worked multiple jobs, traveled the world for pennies on the dollar, and obtained things that perhaps, I could afford but really didn't need only because it gave the "appearance" that I had arrived to some unknown location in life.

What I failed to realize is I was chasing a lifestyle, and missing out on life. While traveling the world, I missed milestones in my kids' life, maybe nothing major like their first step or first word, but perhaps that one day they needed their mom because they had a bad day or even the day something great happened and I wasn't there to share that moment. Though I thought I was doing a noble thing by traveling to make money or working to provide material and mandatory things that my kids needed and wanted, what made me any different than the absent father I had or the mother who consistently neglected me.

Don't get me wrong, I work hard at multiple things now, but my motive is different and my rationale has changed. Yes, I could be making a lot more money doing other things, especially with my qualifications and experience, but now all of the things that I do, I do it for the love and not for the money. Now, even though they are grown, I refuse to miss out on my family occurrences because they give my life meaning. I make a practice to keep my expenses to a minimum so that I never have to chase money or materials, but I enjoy what I have. I believe that this freedom is the life that God spoke of when he mentioned having that more abundant life.

No, I am not a millionaire (yet, by faith), but I do believe that I have the mentality of a millionaire because I don't want to be rich; I want to be wealthy with assets that I can lay aside for the generations to come in my family.

Lifestyle + Occurrence = Life Changing Experience

Definitions

- occurrence- the action, fact or instance of occurring
- experience-the process or fact of personally observing, encountering or undergoing something

Reconciliation

There are occurrences that happen in our lives that divert us from our normal lifestyle or way of living. As you have read thus far, there are a number of changes in my life from rape, to molestation, to promiscuity, to divorces, and the like. All of these occurrences changed my lifestyle drastically.

The rape took my innocence, the molestation took my normalcy, the promiscuity could have taken my life, the deaths could have killed me, the births could have ruined me, the marriages could have changed me and the failed relationships could have broken me. In all of that as I am writing, I hear a, "But God!"

Be it good or bad, experiences come to change us and rearrange us. I often think of the beatitudes that are found in Matthew 5:3-10. I like to have my own version;

Jesus Said	
Blessed are...	
Beatitude (Cause)	(Effect)
The poor in spirit	For they inherit the Kingdom of Heaven
They that mourn	They will be comforted
Meek	They will inherit the earth
They that hunger and thirst for righteousness	They shall be satisfied
Merciful	Obtain mercy
Pure of heart	See God
Peacemakers	Called children of God
Those persecuted for righteousness sake	Thiers is the Kingdom of Heaven

Jennifer Said...	
Blessed are...	
Beatitude (Cause)	(Effect)
The flexible	They bend but they don't break
The bent	They will see the world from a different perspective
The Open-minded	They keep options open
The Sober minded	They will never be blindsided
The Blindsided	They are forever on alert
The Broken	Remain humble to ensure it doesn't happen again
The Positive	For the position themselves for greatness
The reflective	They will always reflect and position themselves to do better.

All of this is just another way of articulating the old adage that says, "When life gives you lemons, make lemonade!"

Writing this book has allowed me the understanding and revelation that the occurrences that have happened in my life may have changed my lifestyle in one way or another, but it was just an experience, not a handicap.

Many times we take our life changing experiences and create a disability because of them. Let me be the first to say that your life changing experience was just that. It was an occurrence that happened in your lifestyle that was divinely orchestrated to change your perspective about a matter. During this process, I believe that I was catapulted into a new way of thinking. I literally went from victim to victorious. I went from "woe is me!" to "Whoa, look what God did for me!" If I ever doubted God's love for me, writing this book has made it evident that my Savior loves me with an undying love.

Life-Changing Experiences vs. Life-Altering Experiences

Definitions

- Change-to make the form, nature, content, future course, etc. of something different from what it is or from what it would be if left alone.
- Altar-an elevated place or structure, as a mound or a platform, at which religious rites are performed or on which sacrifices are offered to gods, ancestors, etc.

Reconciliation

It is important to know the difference between life-changing and life-altering. Life changing experiences, I believe, are designed to change your perspective, but life altering means an occurrence that is out of your control that will forever change your life as your know it.

Sometimes and occurrence can be both. For instance, my mother's death was a life altering experience. However, the way she treated me was life changing. How do I come to that conclusion? Her death was out of my control and there was nothing that I could do about it, but learn to deal with it. However, the way she treated me, I could do nothing about that either, but it changed the experiences that I had and still have with people at times. Her treatment towards me changed my ability to trust, my ability to love, as well as my ability to relate with people. These are all matters that I can and did change and control.

I challenge every person that I encounter to reevaluate the current issue that they may be having. Decide whether it is life changing or life altering and act accordingly.

If it is life changing; look for the lesson, learn it, embrace it and keep it moving. If it is life altering, accept the occurrence and find ways of progressively moving forward within the change that was out of your control. Notice the relationship in the effects of these matters.

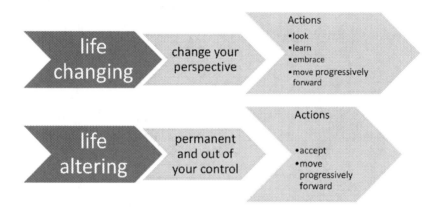

Yes, my rape and molestation changed my life but it made me place that portion of my life on the alter and leave it there. After all, I couldn't do anything to bring back my virginity. I couldn't take those years back that I was forced to "babysit" for a man who just had his way with me. Nothing could be done with that but heal, and that healing came from the hands of the Lord and him alone. I can't even say that if my offenders were to apologize, that it would give me the wholeness that I feel today at the hands of the Lord.

My Lord vs. My Master = My Reality

Definitions

- Lord-the title given to God or Jesus Christ

- Master- The person or thing that has authority, control or power over others.
- Reality-something that exists independently of all other things and from which all other things derive

Reconciliation

I remember one time hearing a sermon by my friend Sarah Jakes Roberts who had talked about how Obadiah, a man in the Bible who was having a conversation with the Lord (in the form of Elijah) and the Lord told him to go and tell his master to free him and that this same master no longer had control over him. This word was so profound because it forced me to embrace the reality that I have allowed my master (my past) to out speak my Lord (faith). Yes, there were times where my situation, (I felt) extended beyond my faith. I felt like my issue wasn't in the Bible and that maybe, perhaps, God was punishing me for some act that I had done or maybe, I didn't do. Nevertheless, it wasn't long before I realized it was all by divine assignment and that those issues that I was experiencing or had experienced had become the master over my life and I made it my reality when it shouldn't have been.

This book has forced me to see my reality, which is I had some life changing experiences as well as some life altering experience and everything that I went through was designed to take me closer to the Christ, because everything that I went through was on the cross. When I resolved to let those things die, I was allowed to live again and enjoy the freedom that Christ had designed for me to enjoy.

When we grasp the reality that we somewhat create our reality, I believe, that we will all be made the better. While writing this book, I realized that I made myself a slave to the master of my past. Due to this captivity, I never fully embraced the freedom that My Lord (Jesus Christ) had created for me. The Bible says, "Whom the son sets free is free indeed." However, as with all promises of God it is contingent upon whether or not we will embrace what he gave us as the gift. In Isaiah 61, it speaks of what I call, "The Great Exchange" that we must all partake in, but it is still within our will. He promised us beauty for ashes, joy for mourning, and a garment of praise for a spirit of heaviness.

The word "for" has several meanings but in this case contextually, it means in exchange for something else. Why do I stress that? I'm glad you asked! The answer is because in an exchange you can't receive one without releasing the other. For far too long and for far too many of us, we have been enslaved to the Master of our past and thought that just because we were moving meant we were over it and moving forward. Well, can I just tell you that movement is not always progressive and that it goes both ways?

Here is an analogy to make it easier to understand. If a child is in the third grade but functions academically at a first grade level, however his or her school pushes them through the education system by consistently promoting them to the next grade, they are moving forward but not necessarily progressing. Actually the skill gaps are only getting larger and it is only a matter of time before the student grows frustrated and taps out of the educational experience all together.

Progressing your reality means that you must free yourself from the enslavement of the master you call your past and move forward with the Lord in headship over the matter. Only HE can heal, only HE can set free, only HE can deliver you from the bondage that, in all actuality, you put yourself in, or that you empowered others to keep you in.

Experience + Revelation =Expectation

Definitions

- Experience-the process or fact of personally observing, encountering or undergoing something)
- Revelation-God's disclosure of himself and his will to his creatures
- Expectation-the act or state of looking forward or anticipating

Reconciliation

My experiences, both good and bad, have afforded me the opportunity to combine my revelation and rationale behind those experiences and make a great reconciliation. This reconciliation is that the same God that brought me through those things can and will bring me through anything else that I may face for the remainder of my life.

I am learning to no longer walk in fear of what may happen, but to walk in expectation that whatever I have been chosen to endure was allowed by God. Does this mean that I never get in my feelings? No. But what it does is give me the assurance that I really can do all things through Christ who strengthens me.

Expectation + Exploration = Manifestation of Revelation

Definitions

- Expectation-the act or state of looking forward or anticipating
- Exploration-an act or instance of exploring or investigating; examination
- Manifestation-to make clear or evident to the eye or the understanding; show plainly

Reconciliation

Another lesson that I have learned through this "journey" is that when I operate in expectation, I am pressed to explore ways and measures of ensuring things happen which brings about the manifestation of the revelation. See if I expect a thing and I explore ways of making it happen, then I open the door for manifestation to come to pass. This is putting actions to your faith. The Bible does say that "Faith without works is dead" So put your faith into action now.

My Reality vs. My Relationship

Definitions

- Reality-something that exists independently of all other things and from which all other things derive
- Relationship-a connection, association, or involvement

Reconciliation

Oftentimes many of us intertwine our relationship with Christ with the reality of our situation. We feel as though, we are going through a thing because he is punishing us for doing such and such. This is not true in the least bit.

Here is the clearest analogy that I can use. I am the daughter of my dad. My relationship with him is the same no matter what I do. If I rob a bank, I am still his daughter; however, I still have to face the consequences of my actions.

The reality of the matter is that I committed a crime and that crime comes with consequences, but it doesn't change who I am.

So it is with Christ. As you have read in this book, I have made many mistakes in my life, but one thing that has remained consistent is my relationship with Christ. No, it did not cancel the consequences that I had to face but my relationship that I have with him made my reality more bearable and he gave me the grace and the strength to face the consequences of my actions. This is why we should praise him in advance for the new grace and the new mercies that we see daily.

Reconciliation vs. Revelation

Definitions

- Reconciliation-to ring into agreement or harmony; make compatible or consistent
- Revelation-God's disclosure of himself and his will to his creatures

Reconciliation

For many years I walked around with unforgiveness of not just other people, but also of myself. I was a walking, talking, preaching, singing and working unforgiveness machine. It didn't take long for God to reveal to me that if nothing else, I was obeying the commandment that says to love your neighbor as you love yourself (Mark 12:30-31).

I wasn't partial in my unforgiveness; I was actually very consistent with it. When I really stopped to look and analyze the situation, I realize that my unforgiveness was bigger than me. It was actually a generational curse from the lineage of my family, on both sides.

Sometimes, even to this day, while talking to my dad, my spirit senses some unforgiveness towards my mom. I hear some unforgiveness from my brother towards my dad and vice versa. When my aunts on my mom's side used to get together, even they use to bicker over things that happened in their past. Seeing all of this dysfunction added to my own inner issues. Unforgivenesss became a learned behavior that was rooted in the core of my DNA.

God literally had to uproot that thing and reveal to me the height and the depth of unforgiveness. The height of unforgiveness is forgiving others, because you have to do that to find the favor and forgiveness in the heavenlies.

The depth of forgiveness is the ability to forgive yourself, despite how you feel in the core of your being. Forgiving ourselves is not a superficial act, but should be a time of self-evaluation. A time to ask questions such as,

"What part did I play in this offense?"

"What could I have done differently?"

"How would I react if that thing occurred again in my life?"

… And being honest about it in your responses.

Divine Revelation

I wish I had the time to share all of my reconciliations and revelations from this journey, but that's a whole other book. The truth of the matter is that I am still reconciling things even now.

28

ACCOMPLISHMENTS- THE LAYERS OF MY BEING

Foreword by A close friend

I have known Lolo for almost 8 years. I know her to be many things, a singer, a comedian, a mother, a true child of God and lastly a friend. My perception of Lolo is that she is a strong person. She has endured many hardships in her life, but she doesn't give up, she trusts God, lowers her head and tunnels through. My greatest concern for her was when she left the church that we attended and worshiped together was. Because I saw her nakedness, her vulnerability and her shame. I thought that surely this was the straw that would break her. I was proudest of her when she had finally finished her CD. She was as proud of her accomplishment as was I. She was in a really good place in her life. When I see or think of Lolo, it ALWAYS makes me smile, even sometimes laugh out loud!!! Because she is such a fun person to be around, you can't be in her presence and not have something to laugh or smile at; she won't let you be down in her presence. She is such an encouraging person; she can take a licking and turn it into something that thrusts her further into learning more about herself and the situation. She immediately gives God the praise and will still be encouraging someone else. If I could speak into Lolo's life I would tell her that she is worth it!!! She deserves it!! When the enemy tries to tell her that she isn't worth anything or that her labor was for nothing, I would love be the one to crush the enemies head!! Yes, Lolo you are worth it, deserve it.

The Journey Continues...

Without a mom, without a dad, without a cheerleader, sometimes without any earthly inspiration, but I made it through the grace of God. People ask me all the time what drove me to the degrees, the books, the cds, the career and all of the many other things that I do, especially when no one in my family on either side has accomplished any of these things. My response is always this, "I cannot help the drive and desires of my kindred, but I always knew I was one of my kind." My mother was one of 6 girls and they all chose their own roads in life. Five of the six of them had children, and we all have chosen our own roads in life but, most of us are all career driven and many are entrepreneurs.

We, as cousins, did all of that without...! We had no role models for the businesses that we are in, we are all believers in Christ and we all have our own story to tell. We have one aunt left and I just believe that that she was left here with us to enjoy seeing the lineages continue and blossom. I know there are times that I look at our family tree and marvel at the greatness of God and the favor that he has over our lives and in our family. The most powerful thing is that we made it without....!

Years ago, I wrote song entitled, "You Have No Clue." I was inspired to write this song because many people THOUGHT they knew me, and they felt that they could handle me any kind of way because of that fact or shall I say that assumption. Many people look at my accomplishments and think that they want to be me, but they fail to count the costs of the oil of this anointing on my life.

God has graced me to make this life of mine look easy, but walk a day in my shoes and see the complexity that is me. There are things that I have been through and sacrifices that I have had to make that have even made me second guess my own self purpose and destiny though I know that I know that I know what God has called me to do. I urge you today to stop looking at the lives of others and desiring to be them because clearly there are some hidden sacrifices that had to be made and so it is with you in your life. What sacrifices are you willing to make to be all that God has called you to be?

Sometimes God's elevation of you and your life makes others uncomfortable. Their discomfort is what produces the behavior that we call "hating." Can we look at the revelation of this term? First of all "hating" comes from a place of jealousy and discomfort. Jealous at the fact that you dare to be different and discomfort in the fact that because you chose to take the path to excellence, it is the manifestation of the choice that they made to stand still.

Don't allow others to make you feel some kind of way because they are uncomfortable. When people used to persecute me for my educational accomplishments, I would allow it to get to my spirit and I would find myself dumbing down my personality to not look as smart as God has blessed me to be. I remember one conversation with a Bishop and he spoke words that changed my outlook. He said to remind people that there are still seats in the school house for them. The seats are comfortable in class, but the outcome creates a comfort that can't be taken away, and that is the knowledge that you acquire that will keep you from your current place of discomfort.

Divine Revelation

The paragraphs above are excerpts from my devotional book 365 Revelatory Words for Any Given Day. I chose these few devotionals because these are words that God have me to encourage myself as David did. Please know that God is no respecter of person and all that he has graced me to accomplish, he will grace you to do the same.

29

WHO I HAVE BECOME

The Dichotomy of Being Moma's Girl

She wanted me, but didn't know what to do with me.

She had me, yet never appreciated who I was.

She caused me my greatest pains, yet taught me my greatest lessons.

She used and abused me, yet made me one of the strongest people I know.

I never understood her love, she never understood my ambition.

I vowed never to be her, but she was also a source of inspiration for me.

Being a mom is the hardest job ever, but yet it is the most rewarding.

I never seek to disrespect nor dishonor her or her legacy, but I had to share my truth.

PREACHER

Chapter Foreword by (my brother)

I have to say it brings me so much joy every time I hear my sister preach. I smile with joy and cry tears of happiness to know that after all that she has been through, she has grown into this remarkable woman, mother, grandmother, sister, friend, and most of all vessel for God and I will love her for an eternity.

How/Why Did I Become A Preacher?

Called at a very early age in a Baptist Church in a time when female preachers were unheard of and especially a child prodigy. Then progressing to go to a Protestant Church while in Europe and then Baptist, A.M.E., Pentecostal, COGIC and finally nondenominational in Georgia, I was exposed to a plethora of religious experiences. I call it adding to my religious toolkit for success.

On the flip side of the coin it also made me a bit spiritually confused because there were so many doctrines and traditions that were taught throughout this sequence.

Due to this occurrence, I wanted God to reveal himself to me and that was my prayer for many years. As God began to reveal himself to me I became more and more thirsty for knowledge of him in a greater way than just knowing the God of my mom and my other family members. This is what led me to pursuing my doctorate in Christian Education. I wanted to learn the authentic truth of religiosity and experience it in its purest form.

This experience not only taught me religiosity, but more so the importance of a relationship with Christ. I was now over the traditions that no one could explain or understand. I couldn't stand the teachings that were being articulated to keep people bound and enslaved to a truth that was not their own.

I now realize that I was called for such a time as this. A time when people are leaving the church, but not leaving God. A time when people are leaving the assembly to reassemble themselves from what we call "church hurt." I am called for a time to tell the untamed truth no matter how much it hurts.

Divine Revelation

I realize my calling and anointing. It is to tell the truth no matter the persecution that follows it. I learned this through my experiences of my rape and molestations and even the abuse when I told the truth and was further victimized for it. Now I have become an advocate for truth tellers and I speak on behalf of those that are afraid to tell the truth for fear of the repercussions that follow. This is what a true trailblazer is.

31

SINGER

How/Why Did I Become A Singer?

Many people may ask what is the difference between a singer, worship leader and a recording artist and why list all three. Though they all deal with music they are three very different entities. A Recording Artist is one who has recorded commercially and sold their merchandise as a means of income. A worship leader is one who evokes the very presence of God and creates an atmosphere that is conducive for the spirit of God to move on the hearts of the people. A singer is one who can sing any genre of music, and just enjoys the art of music and entertains people.

For a season, I would travel with my business partner "The Musician" and I would sing the blues with them as well. I have also sung background for a number of other artists that were not so much in the gospel genre of music. The versatility of my craft is what makes me a singer. Another avenue that falls under being a singer is my ability to provide voice lessons for others in any genre of music to teach them how to develop their craft and use it in a manner that will produce longevity in their vocal gifts.

As a singer who has damaged my vocal cords and had multiple surgeries on my throat from my teenage mistakes of swallowing a blade to stay out of trouble for fighting. I am not supposed to be even be talking now, let alone singing. I show people how to overcome some vocal challenges and still be effective in their craft.

Divine Revelation

Looking at this chapter allowed me to see how I became an asset to the musical community. Not that I do it for that, but music is one of the most therapeutic mediums in life ever. Being able to articulate your feelings through music is the gas pedal to healing when done appropriately. So sing on my friends and let the healing begin.

32

Mother

Chapter Foreword by My daughter

My mother is a great mother and is my best friend. I wouldn't change anything because we all learned together.

Chapter Foreword by my son

I have always seen my mom motivate herself just as much as she motivated others. She kept God and her children first no matter what in life she went through. I think that it is through this mindset that she was able to do all things well.

Being a mom is the greatest honor that a woman can ask for. It does not come without challenge, but at the end of the day, I always say that my children saved my life. They taught me what unconditional love is.

I always wanted to have children to right the wrongs that were done to me. In my own way, I wanted to show my mom how to do it right. For that reason, I became the overachieving parent that I was. In no way am I saying that I got it all right, nor was I perfect at it, but what I did do was not only raise my own children right, but I also raised a number of foster children right. I have a love for children that cannot be explained. I want to advocate for them and help them be the best that they can be.

Divine Revelation

In the raising of my children, I have learned that there are things that my mom did right and then there are things that she could have improved upon. This truth remains relevant for all of us. Many of us place unrealistic expectations on some people and I realize I placed unrealistic expectations on my mom to give me something that she clearly never had. I wanted her to give to me from a place of deficit in her life. Unfair, but true!

33

COMEDIENNE

Foreword by Lolo's Coworker/Fan

Lolo is such a fun loving person. She is so kind and very funny. I have the distinct pleasure of working alongside of her every day. She makes me laugh consistently. She has the ability to focus on small details and find humor and things that most people don't even notice or pay attention to. She is so well versed and imaginative. Not only is she a very serious educator but she is also a comical educator. People love to hear what she is going to say next. She is very jovial and she makes the environment around her very enjoyable. I absolutely love her personality and her energy is contagious. I find myself thinking about her jokes later on in my day and laughing again. She is absolutely fun to be around. At any given time, you can find people in her classroom just because they want to know her thoughts and opinions. She definitely knows how to put a smile on your face. It's very difficult to be sad around her because of her radiant aura. She is so genuine and her and is sincerely one of the funniest comedians I have ever met. I literally have tears from laughing so hard from her comedic jokes. She will bring any event, venue, or arena to another level of laughter.

How/Why Did I Become A Christian Comedienne?

Many people look at comics and think that they are always funny. The truth of the matter is that comics are often the most pained people. They are people who have been through some of the most tumultuous times in their life and often use comedy as an outlet or a refuge from their reality.

Even through comedy I teach the lessons that I have learned about church and will even proceed into making propositions with leaders to create special ministries such as the "Shut Your Mouth" ministry or the "Need a Minute for a Mint" ministry. I can definitely pack a house. I don't just do it for money, but also for charities and organizational fund raisers.

Divine Revelation

Comedy has been my getaway in times when I couldn't afford a vacation. The sad part is that many people didn't know how to segment my personality, so for a season I chose to put comedy down and live life on a serious note, only for a season.
During that season I realized that it was a part of my calling, because I was so miserable when I could not partake in my comedy outlet.
Little did I know that I couldn't expect people to do something that I hadn't done myself. For the longest time I lived life out of balance and could not separate one entity of myself from the other. I soon had to learn it, and learn it quickly, so that I could function and flourish in the fullness of who I am that God could be glorified for the many gifts that he blessed me with.

34

RECORDING ARTIST

How/Why Did I Become A Recording Artist?

I think the original desire stems all the way back to my home church days, but was cemented in my mind in Germany at my 6th grade graduation, my first public performance.

I initially started recording with other artists, but knew that a season had come for me to step out on my own. I had traveled the world and sung with everyone else and now it was time for me to do me, so to speak.

I was working at a Teen Center and we were doing different community events to save our center and one of the people who reached out was a local producer. The children had told him that I could sing and he came by and wanted to hear me. I was so apprehensive about the idea because life had made me begin to question myself. I remember I told him that I could sing anything, but I just could not and would not write anything. He immediately told me that writing would be the first thing that I did.

One thing that I loved about him was the fact that he was my original cheerleader. Everything that I told him I wanted to do, his response was always the same, "What's stopping you?" I never was crazy enough to come up with an excuse, so I just felt compelled to step out on faith and try it. It was under his tutelage that I put my hands to so many different things.

I started writing songs as well as singing them. I started my own clothing line. I wrote my first book. The list goes on and on. The first real solo CD became a mantra for my life Then after that I teamed up with "The Musician" and recorded a full length cd and this year I am releasing two full length cds and there are many more to come. My goal is to do a cd every other year.

Divine Revelation

I believe the biggest lesson that I learned throughout my recording days is that, it takes a special relationship to make special music. There has to be a divine connection between the parties involved. My first producer pushed me to music while "The Musician" made me shut down and never want to sing again. My first producer promoted me while "The Musician" put me down. The first producer made me ask the question of, "Can I Just Be Me?" while "The Musician" made me question, "Does love REALLY cover all? Thank God I found my own voice in my "Journey Back to Me" CD.

35

Worship Leader

Chapter Foreword by my late worshipping partner in crime

Lolo (lil' loc sis is my name for her) is one of the baddest worship leaders I know. This woman can make you instantly go into a worship tangent. With her and the right musician, she can take you into a place of worship that you have never seen, but will make you seek that place for the rest of your existence. I have learned so much about the industry from her. We called ourselves, "Gospel's Greatest Secrets." We often joke about how we are going to be exposed when we get to heaven and that is when the earth will realize what a force we were. I love Lolo and everything about her from her personality to her music abilities, she is definitely my sister from another mister, friends beyond death do us part.

How/Why Did I Become A Worship Leader?

Worship has always been my hiding place. It is the place where I know that I am loved no matter what I am going through. I became an avid worshipper as an adult because it is when I got the revelation of who God is. It also taught me that my relationship with him is more than just attending churches on Sunday, but more so my day to day encounters with him. There is no way in the world that I could have become who I am today, nor be where I am in him today, without worship.

Becoming a worship leader is something that I never really desired to do, but over the years I have become known for my ability to bring people into the secret place with me. Worship is a sacred place where people can come and forget all of their problems for just a moment. Perhaps maybe they don't forget, but it is the place where they can reflect on all God has been to them thus far and remember that the same God who brought them through that can bring them through whatever current state they are in. That is my secret.

Divine Revelation

*Please understand that there is a difference between a worship
leader, which I am, and a spiritual cheerleader which I am not.
A worship leader is a person who embraces worship as a lifestyle,
and not an occurrence. Worship is not something that you do,
but who you are. Spiritual cheerleaders are the leaders who find
themselves leading a spiritual aerobics class. This is done by playing
on the emotions of the people where you find yourself working
hard, leaving people too exhausted to embrace the word when it
comes forth. Worship leaders till the grounds of the hearts of the
people allowing them to receive the word and allow it to take root
so that the people have something to hold on to for the week and
for life. This is who I am, a worshipper with a worshippers heart.*

36

YOUTH MENTOR

I became a youth mentor because I wanted to be to others what I wished someone was for me. Every job that I have held in the professional arena has involved children in one manner or another.

Within these structures I became like a big sister/mom to many teens and young adults. The safe place that they could come to with their deepest of secrets. With groups like the sister's circle, to the young adult Yaya Sisterhood, I believe in building young people up because unfortunately, many times, their parents, often times, don't understand the pressures that our youth today are under. I desire to be the safe place for others that I only wish I had.

Divine Revelation

Even I have been guilty of telling children that because they don't have a job, they don't have no worries. In today's age, that is not in the least bit true. Standardized testing, regular homework and classwork, home life and social media are all stressors in the lives of children. Take the time to listen to children and see things through their eyes. Notice a difference in them, get to the root of the matter, and become and ally and not an enemy.

37

PAGEANT WINNER

This chapter of my life, I owe all to my daughter. She would always tell me how pretty I was, and as bad as I wanted to believe her for one reason or another I couldn't. She went to church one Sunday without me and this happened to be the same Sunday that a group of plus-sized pageant winners were there. My daughter saw them and couldn't help but run home to tell me about it. All she kept saying was, "Momma, if they won, I know you can win!" I refused until I looked into her eyes and saw she really wanted me to do this.

I made a deal with her that said, "If you can find time in my schedule, I will compete." In my mind I was thinking that I was booked to capacity and had no time for something like this. Of course by the grace of God she found a hole in my schedule and booked me for the competition. I couldn't believe it. My daughter did this all by herself. She got with the other queens, told them her feat and they chipped in and helped her get it all done. Before I knew it, I had competed in the local pageant and won, and then I went to the state pageant and got first runner up.

I couldn't believe it, I wasn't even trying. In fact after spending a weekend with these divas, I decided I wanted nothing more than to LOSE this competition because I am a country girl who eats with her fingers when appropriate. I had a habit of saying what I want to say and however it came out was what it was and oftentimes it was not very queenly.

I remember sitting in the interview portion of the competition and they asked the question, "What do you hope to gain by becoming Ms. Texas Plus America. I had no clue because honestly it wasn't my desire.

Before I could even think of what to say, I told them, "If my beauty is what gets me in the door I want to allow my brain to keep me there!" I think that was the question that nailed it for me. When I gave my response many of them had ooohhs and awwwess to say about it, one judge even snapped her fingers.

When we reconvened and it was time for the competition, I just knew I had lost because there were some truly beautiful girls in this competition. When I started noticing everyone leaving but me, my stomach was in knots, not because I wanted to win but because I kept thinking of the million and one other things that I had to do and pageantry was not one of them. They got down to the last three of us and I wanted to cry because I was so upset that my daughter had done this to me. When it got down to the nitty gritty, I got first runner up and that was too close for comfort for me so I never ran again, but I still act as the beauty queen I was crowned to be.

Divine Revelation

I understand that though it was not my desire to compete, what my daughter did for me was crucial. It took the divine revelation for God to show me that it was not about the competition, but about the confidence that the competition showed me that I had. God's favor is what got me crowned because I never gave any effort when there are other ladies who devote a great amount of their lives preparing for events such as this. This was all a part of my journey to give me the validation in my appearance that I never knew I really needed.

38

MODEL

Modeling was something that I always wanted to do. I'm not sure why, but I believe it was a cry for my confidence that my mother kept under her feet. I know now that I used to be a sucker for anyone who said I was pretty.

I remember a modeling school had visited my middle school and high school campus. When they came to my middle school, my parents said no because they were paying for my brother's senior year expenses and I understood as best I could.

When they came to visit my high school, we went to a consultation and my parents filled out the financial aid application and I never heard anything else.

When I got on my own, my daughter and I modeled together. It was great and such a fulfilling pleasure. When I got pregnant again and I endured the mental abuse of their father, I lost my confidence again. I regained it while launching my career as an author and solo artist and then into pageantry which really boosted my confidence more than I knew.

Divine Revelation

I now realize that not only did God grace me with an outer beauty and an inner beauty, but most importantly a beautiful heart.

239

39

AUTHOR

Foreword by Lolo's Bossman

I can offer only the highest recommendation for Lolo. An individual who has extra ordinary reading and writing skills. Once you read one of her books, you will see what I mean!

How/Why Did I Become an Author?

I remember as a little girl my mom was always saying that she was writing a book. I remember seeing her with a huge spiral notebook that she was always writing in. She never put it in to publish and I have no idea of telling you where the spiral notebook is for me to publish it for her.

After finishing seminary, I was always asked to come and to do workshops in reference to church culture and membership. I was a single mom again so I could no longer travel like I was before, so I decided to write a book. It was my first book and I loved everything about the writing process, from the writing to the publishing. The only shock that I was not prepared for was the cover mock ups.

I remember that I had anxiously waited for the arrival of the cover. Finally the day had come. The email was there. I ran and told my daughter who was in her bedroom studying. She came running back with me and we opened up the email and I saw the cover. I was mortified. I couldn't believe my eyes, "A sheep???" Yes, it was a sheep. I remember balling crying and my daughter ran to her room and tried to come up with another concept for the cover. I immediately called my publisher in tears. They assured me it was for the best marketing for the book. They told me that most first time authors don't put their pictures on their book because no one really knows them. I bought into it and I'm glad I did. That book went on to win 2 awards. It was unheard of for an indie (independent) author to win an award for their first book.

From that point on I was addicted. Addicted to writing, addicted to my voice, addicted to the power that my voice had based on the reviews. From that point on, I had told myself and the world that I wanted to put out one book every year for the rest of my life. I did just that until life happened. When I entered into doctoral school, I was fighting over my dissertation and all and I dropped the ball.

When I was led to get back to me, I took on the major feat of catching up to my own personal goals. I then decided to put out the 5 books needed to catch me up to my own personal aspiration and life goal. So I started at the top of 2017 and began the journey of putting out 5 books for the year to catch me up.

All of these books will be released in 2017, but promoted and marketed in 2018 with a major launch and tour and from them on; I plan to stick to my personal goal of publishing a book every year.

Divine Revelation

This chapter is for all of the people who, for whatever reason, allowed life to halt your hopes and dreams. You were on the path of your personal aspiration and then BAM!! Your train was derailed in some way. Well please allow my story to serve you notice that you too can take a Journey Back to You, and make those things happen. It's never too late nor is your request to God denied. Get busy and move forth!

40

EDUCATOR

Foreword by Mrs. Lolo's Coworker/Fan

Lolo is a wonderful, intelligent, and very capable 3rd grade teacher. I have had the pleasure of working with her and I can say that her professionalism and knowledge is invaluable to our third grade department and the school as a whole. She is dependable, honest, friendly and most of all trustworthy. What I know about her is that she is genuine, and sincere about educating our students. She is so entertaining in her classroom. Any day that you walk in her classroom you can see her and the students engaged in meaningful instruction. From observing her class, you may hear the students singing songs, reading aloud together, playing games that reinforce content covered in class, and many more activities that keep the students wanting to learn more. Lolo is just all around a person that you want to know. She keeps the students and adults laughing with her quick wit and humor. It is very evident that she loves children and adults alike. She is very passionate about life and it is evident in her approach to how she gets things accomplished. I feel very honored to know her. She is reliable and I appreciate the role she plays in my life. I know that God has greater and that the best is yet to come in her life. I can't wait to see her in the future because I know she will be a force to reckon with. She is one that has been chosen to change the lives of others and I am glad to call her my friend.

Education was, is and will always be my passion. From my days with "My first real teacher" to my educators in Europe, to the colaborers for the cause that I work with daily today, educators will always have my utmost respect. I believe that education is the freeing agent that prevents us from the bondage of ignorance.

Education is what took me from just a mom, to an advocate for my son. When I found out about his issues, I immediately began to do the research. Computers were neither as prevalent nor accessible as they are now days, but I utilized all of the resources and agencies that I could find to help me through that storm. My son is a major contributing factor to my career choice.

The original seed was planted much earlier in my life by my favorite teacher, "My first real teacher". I felt that if she could make such and impact on a kid like me and make me forget about all of the hell I was going through at home for the duration of the school day, surely I could pay it forward to the next generation.

I wanted to go beyond grade school though. I wanted to teach people how to live. I wanted people to be free from the religious rhetoric that I grew up in and was exposed to.

Many people think that I attained two doctoral degrees for the prestige or to be an overachiever. No! The truth of the matter is that I got my PhD in Christian Education first because religion/relationship with Christ was my first love. I then realized that the degree was not accepted and honored on my secular job at a school district, which is my other passion and I wanted to teach both so I went and got my Educational Doctorates.

Divine Revelation

Education can take you places that reputation can't. Many people walk around with the mentality that it's not what you know, but who you know. I am one who begs to differ. My belief is that who you know might get you there, but what you know is what keeps you there. A hookup might get you in the door, but if you don't know how to operate, no hookup in the world can keep you there.

41

GRANDMA

This chapter is a dream come true for me. I always wanted a grandbaby, but for some reason I never thought that I would have one. Part of the reason is because my daughter had always vowed that she wasn't going to have any, and my son never seemed really interested in it either.

I remember like it was yesterday when my daughter started acting weird. Things that she used to love to smell like my cooking, was now making her sick. She lived on her own and had begun to hang around even more. She would always find herself crawling in my bed and putting the pillow over her head. Finally, one day she came and told me that she was pregnant. I did all but call her a lie. I made her go and get pregnancy test after pregnancy test only for them all to come back positive. I still didn't believe her. We finally went to the real doctor and he confirmed indeed my life had changed forever.

At first, I was angry because I preparing to move away to Dallas to start a new life and I felt she was doing it to trap me to stay with her, which was impossible because I had already signed the contract for my job and for my apartment. Then I went to worry because this meant she was going to be there by herself and God forbid something happen, I would never forgive myself. My final concern was that I wanted her to finish college as she was about to enter into her final semester of school and I didn't want her to be deterred from that destiny. None of the above happened.

We had a plan. My daughter would finish college and when school was out in December she would come to Dallas with me and have the baby there so that I could be in attendance and help as all good Grammys do.

We both kept our end of the bargain and my love bug was born, weeks after my 40th birthday. Little did I know his assignment had begun before he even came into this world.

My grandson has been a lifeline for me. He has served as my motivation to get on this journey back to me. Unbeknownst to him he pushed me beyond cancer and gave me reason to fight. I remember as a baby he would always go to sleep to the song that I wrote. I wrote that song in honor of my children, especially my son who I had just found out was about to graduate high school when doctors said he never would. This song has transcended time, space, and generations.

This entire book is dedicated to the baby of my dreams "my grandbaby", he is my everything. I didn't think that I could love anything or anyone more than my children, after God of course and then my grandson came and swooped my heart away from them and then became first place after God.

Divine Revelation

Sometimes God can place the smallest thing in our life to change the direction of our destiny. I never would have thought that this little being would be a survival piece for me. He pushed me to the greatness that I thought I had lost through the turmoil that was my life. This was a great responsibility to place on such a little being, but he has the anointing on his life to accomplish the task and uphold with due diligence

42

---·◆·◆◆◆◆·◆·---

ENTREPRENEUR

Chapter Foreword by My daughter

I have no choice on whether I shared my mother or not. God prepared us for it and now it's time. Every time she minsters, she not only ministers to that person or that congregation, but she ministers to herself and her team as well. Sharing is caring right?

Chapter Foreword by my son

I am proud to share my mom with the world so that we can all learn how to be a better person. Honestly, there were days I was jealous of the world. I felt left out at times. I would see my sister being my mom's armor bearer and I was either security or the camera man in the background because I didn't realize that we were all vital to the work of the family business, oftentimes, I just felt like the son.

I remember when I went to Arizona for a season to stay with my dad and I would always see my daughter and mom doing a lot of great things and I felt alone and left out even the more. They had no idea of the abuse that I was enduring, one time in particular when my dad took my braces off with some unauthorized tool leaving my teeth damaged for life. As a result, I began to act out so I could come back home to my mom and my sister. When my dad unexpectedly bought me a plane ticket and sent me home with less than 24 hours' notice, I was hurt yet glad because I knew that I was headed to help my mom help the nation.

I am a different kind of millennial entrepreneur. What exactly does that mean? It means that I love the flexibility of doing a multiplicity of things because it keeps me from being bored. I can honestly say that I love everything that I do.

As with all levels of success, there is always a cost. The cost for me was many relationships. I value my friendships to the fullest because most of them have spanned over a period of years. Loyalty is major to me because I feel that if a friend can still by me through my hectic schedule, then I can stick with them through anything.

The biggest question that I am asked is, "How do I find time to do all the things that I do?" My response is always, "When God graces you to do a thing, and he also graces you with the time and energy to complete the work as well." Furthermore, when you love what you do, it never feels like work.

Time management in my life is critical. I partition my life in such a way that I do things in times and season. Naturally I work on my regular job daily, I write in my down time, but I publish once a year. I sing all the time, but I record every other year. I model in seasons depending on what I have launched in that season. I preach occasionally when called. This is just a glimpse as to how I do it all.

Another difference in my entrepreneurship is the fact that I still keep a full time job as well. I have some remarkable "growing" faith, but I have not reached the pinnacle of faith that enables me to depend on my ministry works alone to sustain my standard of living. My fear is that then it will feel like work. Not only that, but I want people to see my hand as a helper and not a hindrance.

I have been in churches where the Pastor or leaders prematurely come off of their jobs putting their families in danger and they look and depend on their members, not only for the church to survive but also for the livelihood of their families.

Am I a millionaire? No! Do I desire to be? No! I know people may not believe that, but it's true. I love living a life of freedom. With all of my success, I live life with few restraints, besides security here and there and I want to keep it that way.

Is it all easy? No! It is all glorious? No! Does it come with a cost? Yes! It is all worth it? Absolutely!

Divine Revelation

I have learned that money isn't everything but freedom is. This is why the bibles says, "Whom the son sets free is free indeed," not "Whom the son makes rich..." I think this is crucial for many to understand. Entrepreneurship is not for the faint of heart whether it is a full time entrepreneur or even a part time one, but it can be done.

43

Rising Again

From the Ashes of my past, I rise
To the beauty that you see inside and outside of me!
I am good enough, I rise!
I am smart enough, I rise!
I am the best me that God created, I rise!
When he went to the cross, he bore my sins,
Sins of my past, my present, and yes even my future.
Because he died, I rise!
I rise daily to the occasion of being who I am!
I rise daily to the occasion of being my best self!
I rise daily to the occasion of not comparing myself to anyone,
Nor will I continue to allow anyone to compare themselves to me!
The old folks used to say that when I get to the other side,
called heaven, every tub must sit on its own bottom.
Why?
Because you have to talk to God about your death (mistakes)
Your life
(redemptions)
Your ressurection
(how YOU rose form the ashes of your cremations of life)
Make a mistake, but learn from it
Cry your tears, because they are watering the seed for your new growth!
Scream and holler, because it gives voice to your most inner feelings!
Use your voice to speak your experience, someone needs to hear it!

Rise my friends, Rise to the occasion that is you!
Rise to the fears that paralyze you,
Rise to the stressors that show your humanity,
No longer should you seek validation, but
you should long for meditation.
Meditation brings worship,
Worship brings relationship,
Relationship brings commitment,
Commitment brings loyalty,
And loyalty brings love!
I love you friends!
Not more than God, but I love you!
I love you my loved ones, not more than you
should love yourselves, but I Love you
NOW RISE!

Divine Revelation

Rising takes work and effort! Isn't it interesting that gravity just occurs? It takes no effort to fall down and certainly not to stay down, but when you make up in your mind that you want to get. You have to start with work which is making the decision that you are no longer happy, nor content where you are. The second action is deciding what you want to do, sit up or get up. Sitting up positions for you for possibility, but getting up positions you for success.

What Are The Three Steps To Rising Again

1. Decide you will not be held hostage to gravity of your issue
2. Choose to either sit up or get up
3. Do it!

The Rebirth of Lolo

How many times are people born? I remember this question being asked at a conference several years ago but I had to leave the room so I never received the answer that they gave. This question has puzzled me for years. Here is my final piece of closure on the matter.

I think that people are reborn daily. How can I say that? I said this because every day we die to our past experiences. Every day we are reborn with new grace and new mercy. We are reborn to a new perspective of the experiences that we have partaken in.

When I first started this project, I was all over the place. I would write on a chapter and then it would get too hard and so I would jump somewhere else. As I consulted with my team of life coaches, I was advised to not do it that way for closure's sake.

I then sought the Lord and he gave me instruction on the structure of this book. Each chapter is significant to a period in my life with the title. Then there is a foreword for many of the chapters written by an instrumental person in my life for that season. Then I continue telling you about the journey. Every chapter is closed with a divine revelation for that season and that is thing that I learned looking back at that season and is the symbolic for the closure that I needed to complete that chapter in my life never to look back at it again.

This structure and sequence has helped me in so many ways. With each chapter as I wrote I felt the closure in the revelation that sealed the deal and closed the wound.

The Lord told me as well to write the chapters in sequence so that I didn't miss the healing that needed to take place as I closed each chapter. He went on to say that for far too long I have been placing a Band-Aid over an infected wound.

This book was the surgical removal that I needed to pluck the infections out of my life once and for all. There are some chapters that I had to sit in that space for a season. You know when the Lord made me sit in it, because there is so much detail in that part. I tell you what I heard, what I saw, how I felt and how my body reacted to the situation. I knew that there, in that place is where I needed the most healing, but I also learned that thing was infected and something about that experience was consistently manifesting itself in my day to day experience and had to be brought to an end.

EPILOGUE

We are blessed to be a blessing. As I stated before, writing this book was no easy feat, but at the same time, it was the most rewarding conquest that I have ever completed.

It was something to be able to tie the loose ends of my life together to create a lifeline of definition as to why I should keep going no matter what adversity I face.

Now that I have done the work for me, I want to introduce you to the sister book of "The Journey Back to Me" entitled "Embracing the Journey: 40 Days of Filling in the Blanks of Your Life."

This workbook takes you through 40 days of getting to know the inner most parts of yourself. You will be peeling back the layers of your being to rediscover yourself, your goals, and the very elements of your being while walking in a new truth.

I caution you that this work is not going to be easy, nor is it going to be comfortable, but it will be one of the greatest things you have ever done for yourself.

The book is set up into four segments; surface, past, present, and future. The surface work done in the first ten days are just some simple ground works that you will need to complete for later exercises. The past work is done in the second ten days and really digs into the heart of the matter that is you. The present work, in the third ten days, is the work that is a lot more intense and will be hard to complete, if you do it right and be honest with yourself. The future work is more of methods of building yourself back up after the stripping away that took place in the sections before that. You will see excerpts from some of my other books in there that are appropriate for the occasion and will be cited at the end of the assignment.

There are specific directions that you should adhere to as you partake in this journey. They are as follows;

- I encourage you to dedicate a consistent place for you to do the work. In that place, there are a few things that you should have on hand…
    - Journal (for your eyes only)
    - Kleenex (trust me, you will need it)
    - This book
    - Pen, pencil
- I am asking that you spend at least 40 minutes a day on your daily exercises and assignments.
- This journey is outlined for 40 days and I am asking that you do it consistently for the 40 days straight while on a fast.
- I am asking that you commit to a fast of your choice. Fasting from something that is important to you. It does not have to be food, but whatever you feel you need on a consistent basis.

The exercises are broken into two parts. You have your word or thought of the day and then you have your assignment for the day which is called "Step in the Journey". In your journal, I would that you head your pages with the day number because there will be times that the assignment will call for your to refer back to a specific day such as Day Three or Day Four etc.

Without further due, let's dive in…

AFTERWORD

"EMBRACING THE JOURNEY: 40 DAYS OF FILLING IN THE BLANKS OF YOUR LIFE"

Day One

Thought for the day: Who are you?

Step in the Journey:

Look at the hats that you wear and ask yourself what or how you acquired that hat. Some hats are by choice and others were not. This assignment is a prerequisite for a number of other assignments, so be as complete and thorough as you can. This is designed to make you aware of the surface layers that you possess. It is similar to the chapters in the book that talks about who I have become in addition to who I was. (i.e. daughter, mother, sister, student, model, author.)

Day Two

Thought for the day: Who do you want to be?

Step in the Journey:

This assignment is very different and a second layer of skin that we are exploring. Of the hats that you wear in day one, you may find that there are hats you want to wear or maybe you don't for some reason, or maybe there are some hats that you currently wear that you always wanted to wear. This question is more like "What do you want to be when you grow up?" While you're at it answer this question, "Who/what do you want to be at the end of this 40 day journey?"

(*Remember, no one will or should see this journal but you.)

Day Three

Thought for the day: Set your goals and then list the steps that you can take towards your desired outcome.

Step in the Journey:

In your life, what are your goals? List them all, no matter how big or small they may seem. Next to your goals, I want you to write what is keeping you from accomplishing them. BE HONEST! If it is yourself that's blocking you, put that down. No Excuses, just facts! Follow this format while answering these questions;

By the end of 6 months, I want to….

By then end of one year, I want to…

By the end of five years, I want to…

By the end of ten years, I want to…

Before I die, I would like to…

By the end of this journey, I would like to…

Day Four

Thought for the day: Perception, Opinion, Fact

Step in the Journey:

Interview people who know your hats (roles). As you witnessed in my book, I interviewed people for the sake of the foreword of the chapter. This exercise served three purposes. One, it allowed me to see how people felt about me in that time and season, or as that entity of my life. Secondly, it honored the people who are important in my life. Lastly, it allowed me to complete the assignment that you are doing today. It allowed me to see if what they had to say was an opinion, a fact, or their perception of me. Yes, I published it just as they wrote it, but the personal evaluation I did was for my eyes only. If you're stuck on what kind of questions to ask, here is what I used when I interviewed for the book.

Stuck? Let me help!

You can use these questions to guide your writing!

1. I have known Lolo for_____years.
2. I know her to be a_____.
3. My perception of Lolo is that she is_____.
4. greatest moment of concern for her was_____
   _____because_____
   _____
   _____
   _____
   _____.
5. My proudest moment of her was_____
   _____because_____
6. When I see/hear Lolo I think or do_____
   _____.
7. If I was to speak words into the life of Lolo or the Lolo of the era that I knew her I would tell her_____
   _____.

Day Five

Step in the Journey:

Compare and contrast what they (the people you interviewed) say, what you say and where you want to be. Don't sit there and say that you don't care what people say because we all care to some degree. Remember, honesty is the best policy in this journey. If you are not going to be honest for the duration of this journey, you may as well forfeit the promise of the exercise now. See how much actually lines up and you may come up with clues how to better meet your goals.

For instance, if they say you are not nice and you say you are not a people person, then being a great sales person is not going to happen because you will not be effective, but infective and ultimately upset everyone that you meet.

Day Six

Thought for the Day: Where?

Step in the Journey:

Think about where you are and then thing about where you want to be and then list all of the reasons you are NOT there. This differs from day three because today you are just reflecting on why you are not where you want to be and on day three you were answering what was blocking you. Though they are similar, they are very different.

Day Seven

Thought for the day: Prepare to dig in and do the work!

Step in the Journey:

Today is where we did in a little deeper into the life of you. Answer this question, "What are your biggest weaknesses, personal flaws, issues that you have in your life, as you know. Do not state what someone else has to say unless you know it to be true.

- I challenge you to take the four steps of heart R.A.T.E. action
    1. Recognize
    2. Acknowledge
    3. Target
    4. Execute
- Change your perception to echo, "I will believe what God says about me because it exudes through my being into the universe for you to embrace and based on what he says about me, which is what I believe, I will TEACH YOU HOW TO TREAT ME AND I WILL SETTLE FOR NOTHING LESS!

*__Caution__: We are getting ready to dive into some deeper truths that are not always easy. Even when you did the interviews on day four, I hope that you didn't interview people who would blow smoke in your face about how great and wonderful you are because that is not going to help you.

Day Eight

Thought for the day: Affect – Effect = Infect

Without having the personal __affection__ of Christ, you cannot be __effective__ to anyone which means you __infect__ everyone!

- Affect means to act on or produce an effect or change in

- Effect means something that is produced by a cause: result: consequence
- Infect- to affect or contaminate with disease

Step in the Journey:

Look at the hats that you listed on day one and ask yourself if you are affecting the people you come in contact with. Are you affecting their lives in a positive manner or infecting them with venom of bad experiences and negative words? This is a hard exercise, but it must be done as a part of the journey.

Day Nine

Thought for the day: Purpose, Passion, Participation

Step in the Journey:

Look at the hats that you listed in day one. Think about the reasons and rationales that you have for doing those things and ask yourself these questions;

- Am I purposed to do this for a greater good in my life?
- Am I passionate about doing this thing?
- Am I just participating in these things just because…

These are important questions to answer. We know that all things work together for the good so there is no bad answer, there are only honest answers. If you are purposed to do a thing, you do it for a reason to accomplish something greater later. For instance, you are purposed to go to school to obtain a degree or some sort of accomplishment to use later.

If you are passionate about a thing, it is the first thing you think about in the morning and the last thing you think about at night. For instance, teaching to me is my passion. Everything that I do, I find the educational value in it.

If you are just participating in a thing, it is just a time filler and something that you do. For instance in my life, the pageant thing was something that I did just because my daughter wanted me to. Now it did boost my confidence, but it is nothing that I think about on a day to day basis.

Another hard exercise, I know but you can do this.

Day Ten

Thought for the Day: Pulse Check

Step in the Journey:

Today just take a breather and reflect on your journey thus far and see what you have learned, how you have grown and what you plan to gain moving forward.

Day Eleven

Thought for the day: Explore, Examine and Evaluate

Step in the Journey:

Now is the time to explore what you are doing, examine why you are doing it and evaluate whether it is in your best interest to continue or not.

Now is the time to redirect your efforts, free up some of your time that you were just participating in things and redirect that towards your goals and taking the journey back to you.

Day Twelve

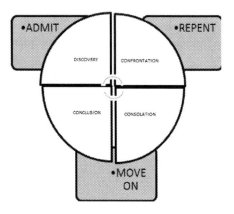

Step in the Journey:

Today is the day that you focus on forgiving yourself for walking in the untruth of who you are. Today is the day that you admit what you did to yourself, repent and move on, never to return to that place of untruth again.

Up to this point in this journey, you may have uncovered some heavy truths that you never realized which brings a new light to the dark places that you have resided. There may have been more than one place of darkness in your life. This is where the DC³ theory comes in. Here is where you take every issue and you discover, confront, conclude and console it. What do I mean? I mean that now that you have discovered the issue (day 1), confronted the issue (day 7, 8), you drew the conclusions in reference to the issue (day 9) now it is time to execute some action (consolation) do something about it. What will your choice be? Are you going to continue wasting time or will you walk in the newness and the truth that you have discovered?

Day Thirteen

Thought for the day: What are some things that I desire for God to change in me?

Step in the Journey:

Answer the above question is the most honest way that you can and even go on to explain why. Is it keeping you from living your best life? Is it forcing you to inflict harm on yourself in any way (i.e. stress, frustration, lack of peace, etc.)?

Day Fourteen

Thought for the day: Reflections

Step in the Journey:

What are three issues in my life in which I need to make sure I use the DC^3 theory (those that I have started but not completed or need to get started on)? For the issues that I have begun working on, what phase of the DC^3 theory am I in?

1. _____
   _____
2. _____
   _____
3. _____
   _____

Day Fifteen

Thought for the day: Acknowledge, Believe, and Control

Step in the Journey:

A- Acknowledge the problem

B- Believe that God can turn it around

C- Control the inclination to submit to the wishes of anyone other than God and yourself.

Today look at all the issues that you have uncovered so far and follow the A.B.C. above. Continue to proclaim this over yourself daily. Not just today but for the duration of this journey. Every issue that you uncover, say your A.B.C.'s.

Day Sixteen

Thought for the Day: I wish!

Step in the Journey:

What are the top five things that you wish people knew about you and why? How do you think it would help them to understand you? Think about the interviews that you done. How would these truths about you affect change on those people's perception of you?

What are five things that I wish that people understood about me?

1. _____
   _____
2. _____
   _____
3. _____
   _____
4. _____
   _____
5. _____
   _____

Day Seventeen

Thought for the day: Place, Process, Project

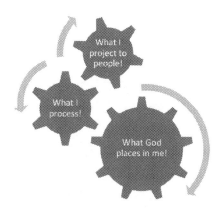

Step in the Journey:

When God places a thing in us for us to do or to become, oftentimes we process his command, but we forget to execute or project it out for people to see in us. Today, I want you to think about maybe, there are some things that God told you to do and you already processed it, but because of whatever reason you have not carried it out. What are those things? List as many of them as you can along with the reasons why. Then I want you to see how can you return to that command and begin to act it out.

Day Eighteen

Thought for the day: 4T-Truth, Transparency, Tenacity, and Testimony

Step in the Journey:

Today I want you to share at least one new truth that you have discovered in this process. Tell them how this transparency is helping you and include in there how you have the tenacity to get back up and get it back together again and use this opportunity as an opportunity to testify. You can choose more than one person if you would like, because the more you share the better you will feel and in all actuality, you will be encouraging yourself to keep going.

Day Nineteen

Thought for the day: Pulling versus Patching

Step in the Journey:

Today I want you to think about the difference that you have made in your life by pulling out and exposing your issues versus placing a Band-Aid over the infected wound and temporarily patching it up out of avoidance. Write out how it makes you feel and reflect on your process and journey thus far. I want you to shoot for writing a one page reflection on your journey thus far.

Day Twenty

Thought for the Day: Pulse Check

Step in the Journey:

Today just take a breather and reflect on your journey thus far and see what you have learned, how you have grown and what you plan to gain moving forward. Notice, we are always projecting forward.

Day Twenty One

Thought for the day: Patient to Provider

Step in the Journey:

Today is the day that you have gone from patient to provider. Did you realize the biggest difference between a patient and a provider is the direction in which they wear their garments? A doctor wears his garments open towards the front symbolizing his/her ability to show their heart concerning the matter. A patient wears their garments open in the back to focus on the issue and to cover the heart of the matter.

By partaking in this journey, you have changed the direction of your garment and you are showing the courage that you have to face your issues head on and realize that we all have issues, but only a few of us are willing to confront them and rectify them to make them better. Pat yourself on the back and take a journey through your journal to see just how far you have come. How do you feel?

Day Twenty Two

Thought for the day: Celebrating Your Freedom

Step in the Journey:

Here are the twelve steps to being free from people and not being in the same position you was in before.

12 F's For Finding You Freedom From People

1. Formally acknowledge the issue
2. Familiarize the location of the offense
3. Find rationale if you can
4. Finish to get a resolve
5. Forgive yourself
6. Forget the offense
7. Forward action toward progress
8. Formulate your personal decree
9. Follow your heart
10. Feed your intellect
11. Forgive others

12. Finalize the funeral

-And Deliver Us From People (2014)

Day Twenty Three

Thought for the day: The death of the people pleaser!

Step in the Journey:

Today I want you to take the opportunity to write the obituary of the person that you used to be. I am going to share with you the obituary that I wrote for myself in my book entitled, "And Deliver Us From People!" Feel free to use any part of it that you would like, but use your words and issues.

The Obituary of the People Pleaser
Lolo, 36 (at the time)

Former resident of People Pleasingville, USA… died
November 22, 2011, at her home in Texas.

At her request, no service will be held.

Ms. Lolo was born January 11, 1975 in Oklahoma to my parents
Lolo could accomplish anything she set her mind to do. At a very
early age, she accepted her call to Christ and to ministry.

Lolo served in the Army of the Lord, during World War I (the
deliverance from family), World War 2 (deliverance from Christians)
World War 3 (deliverance from abuse), and the Desert Storm (finding
her way from religion to relationship) and recently the war on Terrorism
(deliverance from people and herself). In 2011 she spent 10 months
in the wilderness and then went into the cave, wherein she DIED!
Please don't grieve because the story doesn't end there! You see
just like they thought the story ended when Jesus and Lazarus
went to the tomb, but when the others returned to find them

they were not there, Lolo (the people pleaser) is there, but
Lolo the fighter for life (her own life) was resurrected!

She has worked many years for the accomplishments that she has
made and refuses to allow others to make her success her sorrow!

Ms. Lolo spent more than 30 years on Earth. She and her children, my
daughter and son, built their home on the love of the Lord and knew
that together they could survive anything, though the children are
grown and gone, the family enjoyed many wonderful days together.

She is survived by her purpose and her destiny and her
will to live and the processing of her pain through this last
painful perseverance of being delivered from people.

Condolences may be sent to P.O. Box 666,
Hellnation, Lake of Fire 54321-free!
Be blessed and know that the best is yet to come!

-And Deliver Us from People (2014)

Now you try to write your own!

Day Twenty Four

Thought for the day: You have a legal responsibility!

Step in the Journey:

Please review the information below to assist you in the process of you
staying delivered from the darkness of your past.

The Legal System of People Deliverance

1. **Victim/Suspect**- in this phase you have to decide if you are the
   victim or the suspect. Sadly enough we choose to want to become

the victim, but I am sorry my friends you are really the suspect because you failed to execute the power needed to overcome the enemy. You gave into his satanic influence and yielded to his oppression. You allowed people to do what they done to you, no one held a gun to your head and said believe what I say and let it rule your life, you allowed that!

2. **Hearing**-there was a hearing held in your honor to see if there was enough evidence to bring you to this point, being delivered from people and God said, "Yes!" He's heard enough of your whining and crying about the misuse of you in reference to people. No more crying about them. Now he has pulled out the mirror and is forcing you to speak me and my. TAKE ACCOUNTABILITY!

3. **Subpoena**-after the hearing God issues a subpoena to go out and seize the property that belonged to you from others whom you have allowed to prostitute you in such a way that causes you pain and heartache. Remember this has nothing to do with right or wrong, but everything to do with God proving a point to you, about you, for the betterment of you!

4. **Search warrant**-He went into the rolodex of your mind and caused you to remember all of the encounters in which you thought you were the victim, when actually you were the suspect and he brought those memories to the forefront. Having to face the reality is a hard thing to do but when you are forced to face it in this manner, it becomes oh so surreal!

5. **Arrest**-when a person is arrested they are incarcerated or confined to a space for a given amount of time for the purpose of keeping others safe, but more so as a time of reflection or punishment for the wrong actions that they have committed. God brought those memories back and placed them on a platter of your mind and he is making you face the music of your bad decisions and he is giving you the opportunity to prepare yourself for your spiritual due process.

6. **Court**-In the court hearing, evidence is evaluated and petitions are made from both sides of the legal system. In this case there is a divine conversation between you and Christ alone. He is the prosecutor and he allows you to be the judge of your actions and intentions. This allows for the due process to be more meaningful, but you have to first acknowledge what you did for true healing to take place. What I love about this court system is that his order of the court is done in love. He is not condemning you, and will not allow you to condemn yourself, but will show you a more excellent way that will help you to experience the peace that passeth all understanding and the abundant life that he has designed you to encounter.

7. **Conviction**-In the courts of law, there is either a judge or jury that makes the conviction. In this case we are being delivered from the jury so you have to allow the convicting power of the Holy Ghost to rule in this case because he lives inside of you, the judge. Now this conviction is not for condemnation but it's for edification. (God teach me how to do better the next time and how to learn from these experiences never to do this again, inflicting pain on myself while displacing it on others and playing the victim role.)

8. **Sentencing**-As the judge, you make the authoritative decision as to whether or not you will allow this type of injustice to occur again and you will stand in your rightful place and take your life back. In Christiandom, the number eight is new beginnings and that is what this this is. After sentencing, you have the right to move on with a new found freedom and understanding of what needs to be done in your life and how you need to move on with new life lessons and revelations of how to proceed with your life. (…old things are passed away and behold all things are made new!)

-And Deliver Us from People (2014)

Day Twenty Five

Thought for the day: Get Ready for the Metamorphosis

Step in the Journey:

We all know the metamorphosis to be the lifecycle of a butterfly. Where initially as a caterpillar, they take in all the food that they can to sustain them through their cocoon phase. Then they stay in the cocoon for a season before they blossom as a butterfly. Well my friends, now is your time to prepare yourself for the cocoon. We have done a lot of work up to this point and now you are preparing to enter the cocoon. Take this time to reflect on the hard truths that you have encountered in the past three weeks. I know that it hasn't been easy, but today I am asking you for the next 48 hours to go on a complete fast that your flesh may die and your spirit may rise again. You have taken in truths and experiences in these weeks and you have gathered them in preparation for the cocoon. Now you, my friends, are getting ready to enter into the cocoon of your journey. Today, write a reflection and a hope guide of the things that you want God to reveal to you concerning you. What are the things that you have hidden from people, even family, that you know is holding your bound. Write it down as a form of release. Tell yourself how this "thing" or "issue" has affected the freedom that God has designed for you to live in. I cannot stress it enough to BE HONEST! Your life depends on your honesty and no one but you can free you! God designed you to live in freedom and only you can keep you bound. Please take this exercise seriously!

Day Twenty Six

Thought for the day: In Hidden Places

Step in the Journey:

Now that you are in the cocoon, what are the things that you have been hiding? This is the time to expose them. ALL OF THEM!! Write down all of the lies in your life that you have told for one reason or another. I am not talking about the "who ate the cookie, from the cookie jar?" type lies. I mean the ones that you have told to keep you from living your best life. The lies that you know that if people knew them, you think, they may see you differently. For instance for me, it wasn't a lie, but I never told people before that I spent a summer in a mental institution. I also never told people about me sex addiction. These are hidden things and lies that I told by not telling them. You can lie by omission or commission. My lie was by omission. Had I told people I suffered from abandonment issues, maybe they would have handled me differently. Today is the day that I want you to list the lies and also how they have affected you in your life today.

Day Twenty Seven

Thought for the day: Hurt or Heal?

Step in the Journey:

Today is the day that you are going to look back at the list that you made yesterday (Day 27) in its entirety and ask yourself, "Are you going to continue hurting yourself by living this lie, or are you going to heal yourself and tell the truth. I don't mean just run and tell everyone your business, I mean being open and honest and sharing <u>as the Lord directs you to</u>. Even though I put my life in a book, I still only share face to face as the Lord leads because some people will take your transparency and try to use it to keep you bound again. They simply can't handle the truth of who you are, but you can. This decision is yours. Are you going to live healed or continue hurting yourself with your own untruths? How are you going to break free? What is your plan? Who do you need to tell? How will you tell them? What will you do when you see their reaction? Today is going to be a hard day, but you can make it through.

Day Twenty Eight

Thought for the day: Rise or Remove

Step in the Journey:

Another challenging day of decisions this is going to be. Yesterday, you made a huge leap inside of your cocoon by shedding some layers of untruths and sharing them in one manner or another. Today is a new day! Today is the day that you rise to the occasion and realize that there may be some people or some things in your life that you need to free yourself from. I always tell people in my coaching sessions that you cannot take away a thing in your life without replacing it with something. Same thing goes for here. Yesterday you exposed yourself, now people are going to have to rise to the occasion of the new you, and your new truths or you are going to have to remove them from your life. Today, I want you to list the things, people, or issues that you need to rise up, or that you need to remove from your life and do it. Make no apologies, make no excuses. Your life depends on this and so does your journey back to you!

Day Twenty Nine

Thought for the Day: Birth to Rebirth

Step in the Journey:

Reading for the Day: It Was In My Falling!

There is power in falling! In fact that is the most likely time when God will and can step in is when you are down. You have used all your knowledge, used all of your intellect and yet and still the problem is still there. It is when you fall into position that he can manifest his glory in your life. It is not only when you fall, but how you fall, and what you do when you are down there. No matter how you fall if you worship, he will meet you! When you cry out, he will hear you! When you ball up in the fetal position he will rebirth you to where you won't even know yourself when you rise.

Notice I said, "When you rise." I didn't say "if" but "when". This is a guarantee that it is going to happen but you first have to fall. Get into the birth position and prepare for rebirth.

- 365 Revelatory Words for Any Given Day (2017)

Day Thirty

Thought for the Day: Pulse Check

Step in the Journey:

Today, just take a breather and reflect on your journey thus far and see what you have learned, how you have grown and what you plan to gain moving forward.

Day Thirty One

Thought for the day: Know your rights!

Step in the Journey:

Today is the first day of the rest of your life. Now you are beginning to emerge out of your cocoon, back into the new world. Yes, the world may be the same, but your view is going to be different. Why? Because now you are able to see with a new set of eyes, and a new perspective, now it is time to empower yourself with the newness of your existence. Know your rights! You have the right to:

- Change your mind
- To say NO
- To be who you are

These are your new inalienable rights. Walk in them and don't ever forget them.

-And Deliver Us from People (2014)

Day Thirty Two

Thought for the day: Ten Commandments of Freedom

Step in the Journey:

Today I want you to copy and post these 10 steps to make sure that you stay free from the things that once had you bound. Commit these Ten Commandments to memory.

1. Present it to the father
2. Present it to yourself
3. Process your decision
4. Proceed with caution
5. Protect yourself
6. Practice, practice, practice
7. Progression or prostitution, you make the choice
8. Proceed with purpose
9. Promise nothing
10. Permit yourself to make your own decision

And Deliver Us from People (2014)

Day Thirty Three

Thought for the day: Reevaluate for Revolution

Step in the Journey:

Reading for the Day: Where am I?

If you just take a moment, no matter what you're going through and just begin to think of where you could be versus where you are, I promise you that you will find your place of peace and gratitude realizing that it could be worse than it looks. Every year I set personal goals, ministry goals and financial goals. These goals all coincide with my life goals for myself. When I take the time to review the status of my life goals, I ask the question, "Where am I?" This comes when you live life intentionally and on and in purpose. All things that I do in my life should tie right in to my life purpose and destiny. When is the last time that you took the advice of scripture and wrote your vision and made it plain that others may see it and run with you or run away from you? Reevaluate where you are in relation to where you want to be and stay on track allowing nothing to deter you.

- 365 Revelatory Words for Any Given Day (2017)

Today make yourself a set of personal goals, ministry goals and financial goals.

Day Thirty Four

Thought for the day: Walk in 180

Step in the Journey:

Reading for the day: JUST KEEP IT MOVING

This is not the time to stand still, but to move and see the salvation of the Lord. For too long we have cried and whined about how we went through this and we went through that. It is now time to move on from the things that are of the former days and let's just look forward to the days to come. I promise you out latter will be greater than our former because the word of God tells us so. Let's make our next days our best days. Listen, what can you really do about the days that are gone? Nothing right? Just learn from them and keep it moving. Yes, they lied on you, but keep it moving! Yes, they stabbed you in your back, but keep it moving! Yes, you were misunderstood, but keep it moving! Whatever you do JUST KEEP IT MOVING!

- 365 Revelatory Words for Any Given Day

Make a choice today of a few things that you will keep it moving from (i.e. relationship, job, family, church, friends). What is it?

Day Thirty Five

Thought for the day: Just Do It!

Step in the Journey:

Reading for the day: I'm Out!

We, as believers, have to learn when to walk away and when to say, "I'm Out!" My Pastor teaches us all the time about the need to have personal core values in which you live by and how those core values often come from your pain and experience. He went on to teach us that anytime we encounter a person or experience that puts those core values in jeopardy, its ok to say "I'm Out!" My core values are loyalty, honesty, integrity, accountability, transparency and humility. Anytime I encounter someone or something that does not operate in those core values, I have no problem saying, "I'm Out!" This goes for personal, professional, family, or friend relationships. I have a spirit in me that is called the "I'm Out!" spirit. For the longest time, I wouldn't use it because I know what it feels like to be left and abandoned, but when I found my voice, I gave myself permission to remain loyal enough to be true myself and my core values and therefore now I have no problem saying, "I'm Out!"

- 365 Revelatory Words for Any Given Day

Make a list of your five core values!

Day Thirty Six

Thought for the Day: Make Your Choice/ Make Your Change

Step in the Journey:

Reading for the Day: You Don't Have To Stay Where You Started

I don't care where you came from, I don't care what you have been through YOU DON'T HAVE TO STAY THERE. Moving on is a choice that must be made by the individual who will take responsibility for their own destiny. I made up in my mind a long time ago that I wanted to be someone and I wanted to do things that have never been done in my family. Not only did I make this vow but I have some cousins who made the same vow. I have a great family and we have all walked very different paths, but at the end of the day, it is always a joy to sit back and watch us all surpass our parents and want more than what they had. It is a joy to see and it makes my heart glad to know that we all have the same mentality that we will not stay where we started, but we will create a new path for our generation and the generations after us. #Greater works shall you do!

- 365 Revelatory Words for Any Given Day

What is it that you do differently than how you grew up? How does it make you feel?

Day Thirty Seven

Thought for the day: No More Excuses!

Step in the Journey:

Reading for the Day: Purpose, Not Problems

The things that I go through are not really problems when I understand that they are all working toward my purpose. Changing your perspective on the issues of life is all about maturity and growth. This is when a word becomes rhema and revealed in a real way. It is no longer just words on a page, but a reality of life. It's the blessed assurance that we often sing about that says not matter what I do through, I know I serve the same God that brought me out of the last issue to bring me through this one as well. Remember that everything that you go through is all about purpose and preparation for the next level of glory that you are about to experience. So don't curse it, embrace it and know that it all works for your good.

- 365 Revelatory Words for Any Given Day

Think of the worst thing you have been through and recall how God brought you through and what lesson you learned and write it.

Day Thirty Eight

Thought for the day: Quitting the Quest is not an Option

Step in the Journey:

Reading for the Day: Don't Quit!

We all want to quit at one time or another. We feel like what is the use. People quit for different reasons. One is just the fact that they are pitiful. They came into this place with the desire to not complete the task. They didn't believe in themselves from the beginning. Another reason why people quit is because they are in prestigious positions and they feel like they would rather not even try for fear of failing in the public eye. Finally, another reason that they quit is due to personal problems like the proclamations made to them at some point in time. Well I came to tell you that there are solutions for not quitting. God made a promise that he would never leave you nor forsake you. He promised to protect you against every wicked thing that tries to consume you. He also promised provision, so yes you may be limited in your own strength but you are able to make it through if you just trust him. Finally he is putting you in a position where you are successful but he gets the glory. So, quitting is not an option!

- 365 Revelatory Words for Any Given Day

What are three obstacles or oppositions that you have made up in your mind that you won't quit as a result of?

Day Thirty Nine

Thought for the day: It's All About Process

Step in the Journey:

Reading for the Day: There Is a Process to Your Purpose

I'm reminded of a time when my children were smaller and there was a stroller that I wanted soooo bad because it was perfect for both of them to ride in though they were two different sizes. I worked hard to get the money for that stroller, mind you I was 18 years old and they had just come out with these strollers so they were expensive. So I finally got enough money to get one and I was so excited. I couldn't wait to get home and open the box and put my babies in it and go for many walks. Then I opened the box and saw the million and one pieces that was in the box. Now I knew what it was supposed to look like in the end, but it didn't look nothing like it when I took it out of the box. As a much older and wiser person now, I get the revelation of it all. See only God knows what we will look like in the end. What we see right now in ourselves are the million and one pieces that I saw in the box. The beauty of life is when we are being put together piece by piece. There is a process that we must go through in order for us to be polished for our purpose. Whether the pieces were in a million pieces in a box or put together to make this phenomenal stroller that I just paid a lot of money for, it was still a stroller. You are still who God called you to be whether you are in a million pieces or all together you will forever be in the process for your purpose

- 365 Revelatory Words for Any Given Day

Do you feel like you are being put back together again now since the beginning of this journey and how does that make you feel? If not, what else do you need to do?

Day Forty

Thought for the day: Value the Completed Journey!

Step in the Journey:

Reading for the Day: It Is Finished!

Why is it that we compartmentalize the Bible and the occurrences that happened? What do I mean? I am glad that you asked! What did you think about when you read the title of today's devotional? Many people would look at it and think of the seven last sayings of Christ that we have reserved for the Resurrection Season. Others may have looked at it and thought that I was celebrating the fact that this book is FINALLY DONE! There are so many interpretations to this title and the truth of the matter is that it means all of the above mentioned and then some. See I said when I wrote my first book that I wanted to write a book every year for the rest of my life. I did it for three years and then life happened. I was in and out of bad relationships. I survived cancer. I started my secular career in education and did a number of other things. This books is representative of the resurrection of the my call, will, and desire not just for me, but for

Christ. This book serves as my rededication to my craft, my recommitment to my dreams, and when I say it is done, I mean it.

The excuses are done!
The sob stories are done!
The procrastination is done!
The insecurities are done!
The self-doubt is done!
The struggles that I allowed to stop me are done!

Am I saying that I think that I am exempt from issues of life and that the rest is smooth sailing? NO! But I am saying that I will no longer let anyone or anything come between my goals and I again!

- 365 Revelatory Words for Any Given Day

What is finished in your life today? Write a reflection of how you feel today versus day one.

CONCLUSION

After embarking upon this journey back to US, now I am sure that we have all discovered some new truths about ourselves. For me, one of my biggest truths is that fact that I didn't realize how long I lived my life from a place of numbness. I don't know how many times I found myself writing this word while completing this work. I hate using the same word over and over, but I could not find a more fitting word to articulate my issue, so I used that word a lot and I am sure you saw it.

Another realization is that the words that my mother spoke into me as a girl, I still heard as a woman. I learned that long after she was gone, I was still living out the manifestation of the venom that she spoke over me wishing at times it would take me out of my misery, but instead empowering the words with my mindset to make me more miserable.

Due to the abandonment issues that I suffered from, I innately learned to run towards deal breaker responses for every relational issue. As a protective measure, instead of working it out, I ran away. Never being exposed to loyalty and commitment, but a life of infidelity and abuse, I clung to what was familiar, abuse.

Having now done the work, I realize my life is about choices. I can choose to better or bitter, healed or hellish, hurt or whole. I choose to be a better, healed, and whole individual. I urge you not to be encouraged by just my healing, but enjoy the beauty that is my scars. My scars tell a story of their own.

LOLO

I remember when I was telling my doctor that I wanted to write this book, he was strongly against it due to the fact that the treatments that I took while battling with cancer severely affected my memory and the frustration of trying to remember things to write about could produce stress, and stress increases the chances of reoccurrences. Well, I didn't take his advice. I did the work. I may not have remembered every detail, but I remembered enough to get my point across. Now, I walk in a new freedom and a new self-love that I never knew possible.

I hope you all have enjoyed this journey as much as I did. I am grateful to God for you and your support. Thanks again and remember to keep embracing the Journey Back to You!

ABOUT THE AUTHOR

Lolo is a veteran educator, author, singer, model, and a plethora of other things. She has published eight books covering genres such as religion, education, relationships (singleness), and self-help. Lolo has two grown children and a grandson. She lives in Houston, Texas.

Printed in the United States
By Bookmasters